THE
POWER
OF
BECOMING

ACHIEVING PERSONAL FULFILLMENT

PAUL R. MORK

Beaver's Pond Press, Inc.
Edina, Minnesota

ISBN-10: 1-59298-127-5
ISBN-13: 978-1-59298-127-4

Library of Congress Catalog Number: 2005909699

Printed in the United States of America

First Printing: January 2006

09 09 07 06 05   6 5 4 3 2 1

Cover and interior design by Pat St. Claire
Typesetting by Prism Publishing Center

Beaver's Pond Press, Inc.

7104 Ohms Lane, Suite 216
Edina, MN 55439-2129
(952) 829-8818
www.BeaversPondPress.com

To order, visit www.BookHouseFulfillment.com or call 1-800-901-3480. Reseller discounts available.

"In his new book, *The Power of Becoming*, Paul Mork has cut across the traditional lines between parents and children, between coaches and players, between athletes and non-athletes, between the intellectual and the pragmatic. There is truth and encouragement for every reader! Drawing from his rich experience as a highly successful teacher/coach, Paul weaves examples of *Becoming* that touch our hearts while challenging us to examine closely what we are *Becoming* or have *Become*. In my case, this book reminds me of the Apostle Paul describing his life journey in Phillipians 3:12-14."

"Not that I have already obtained all this, or already been made perfect, but I press on to take hold of that for which Christ Jesus took hold of me. Brothers, I do not consider myself yet to have taken hold of it. But one thing I do: forgetting what is behind and straining toward what is ahead, I press on toward the goal to win the prize for which God has called me heavenward in Christ Jesus."

- **JERRY KINDALL** - *American Baseball Coaches' Hall of Fame; former major league baseball player; long-time head baseball coach at the University of Arizona; author of five books.*

"The lessons contained in *The Power of Becoming* apply to almost every aspect of life. This is a book about *Becoming* better than you already are. The author, by God's grace, enthusiastically shares ways to lead an exciting and meaningful life. It is about becoming successful and significant in whatever you do."

- **LES STECKEL** - *President/CEO of the Fellowship of Christian Athletes National Organization; former National Football League head coach; Lt. Colonel in US Marine Corps.*

THE POWER OF BECOMING...

"*The Power of Becoming* is a practical step-by-step guide for a meaningful spirit-filled journey through life. Mr. Mork not only explains how to awaken our inner spirit, but also why we need to do so. Each of us can begin that journey right now, regardless of our current circumstances.

Our journey is simply to *Become* who we were meant to be. God created each of us to be an integral part of life. Once we choose to accept that, we will find meaning, purpose, joy, and so many other of God's little miracles of life. I highly recommend Mr. Mork's book for anyone who wants to *Become* all that God intended for us."

- **JOHN CASTINO** - *Senior Vice President of the Wealth Enhancement Group; former Minnesota Twins' Most Valuable Player in 1980 and 1982; American League Rookie-of-the-Year in 1979.*

"Life is no game. It's for real. And since we only get one chance at making our lives count for something, it makes perfect sense to attempt to discover ways that will improve our chances for successful living. As coach, teacher, husband, father, and grandfather, Paul Mork digs deep into decades of personal experience to share with his reader lessons personally learned. He is a master at the art of encouragement and it is encouragement for living that you'll experience in *The Power of Becoming*."

- **REV. ROGER EIGENFELD** - *Thirty-three year pastor of St. Andrew's Lutheran Church (9,000+ members) in Mahtomedi, MN; founder of St. Andrew's Academy; former member of the Board of Regents of Augsburg College, Minneapolis, MN.*

THE POWER OF BECOMING...

"*The Power of Becoming* is a must-read for anyone looking for a sense of peace, purpose, and meaning in life. Paul Mork skillfully unwraps tremendous insights on how people can become more alive physically, intellectually, and spiritually."

- **DAVID GIBSON** - *Pastor of Missions and Outreach, Grace Church, Eden Prairie, MN; former Executive Vice-President of the national Fellowship of Christian Athletes; former Executive Director/COO, Mission America.*

"*The Power of Becoming* will make a difference in your life and all the lives you have the privilege of touching. It will become an invaluable tool in one's pursuit of excellence."

- **HARRY MARES** - *Former Minnesota State Representative; Chairman of the State Education Committee; former mayor of White Bear Lake, MN; career high school social studies teacher and coach.*

"I know that the concepts and thoughts put forth in *The Power of Becoming* will be used by me as I continue to teach and coach. Mr. Mork brings a fresh perspective and new ideas that we can use in our daily relationships with others. The book teaches and inspires."

- **DON GLOVER** - *Thirty-five-year high school and college educator; former Minnesota Teacher-of-the-Year; Minnesota Cross Country Hall of Fame; teacher and coach at the University of Wisconsin, River Falls.*

THE POWER OF BECOMING...

"Even before writing this book, Paul Mork has influenced thousands of young people with his passion and integrity, both as an inspiring coach and a notable English teacher."

- **JOE KIMBALL** - *Journalist and columnist; former athlete and student; author of Secrets of the Congdon Mansion.*

"Paul Mork cites an amazing breadth of literature and biblical quotations to support his assertion that we all can *Become* much more of what God wants us to be. This book is both inspirational and practical in helping us to make the world a better place. As might be expected from a long-time coach, *The Power of Becoming* is a resounding admonition that it is not whether we win or lose in life, but rather, how we play the game that counts and impacts those around us."

- **DR. DAVID ROSSMILLER** - *Family physician; Christian Medical Association; Phi Beta Kappa, University of Wisconsin.*

"*The Power of Becoming* helps us all reaffirm the gifts that God has given us by claiming us as His own special children. *Becoming* is not a simple task, but one that all are encouraged to explore and acknowledge in all of our human relationships. *The Power of Becoming* gives good insight into reigniting our passion to be all that God intends for us to be."

- **REV. LAUREN WRIGHTSMAN** - *Pastor of Young Families, St. Andrew's Lutheran Church; BA Luther College; M. Div. Luther Theological Seminary.*

Acknowledgements

A special thanks to Pat St. Claire of the St. Claire Design
    Studio for her work on the book's design and
    photography. Pat's insights, creativity, and
    judgment were excellent.

Augsburg Fortress Publishing House
    A number of hymns.

Beaver's Pond Press, Milt Adams - Publisher

Burch, R. Kurt, PhD. - Editor

Manna Music, Inc.
    How Great Thou Art, words and music by Stuart
    K. Hine, copyright 1953, S. K. Hine. Renewed
    1981 by Manna Music, Inc., 35255 Brooten Road,
    Pacific City, OR 97135. All rights reserved. Used
    by permission. (ASCAP)

*D*edication

*T*o my wife, Marilyn Ivonette Mork.
A hard-working, unassuming, loyal partner.
An unsurpassed love for family.
Mamie, my heroine.
Thank you for being an angel on earth.

*A*lso to our children: Pamela Renee, Kyle Dean,
Kimberly Kay, and Heather Lynn.
We are proud of what each of you
have been, are, and are
*B*ecoming.

$\mathcal{T}$ABLE OF CONTENTS

Consider

Is anyone happier
   Because you passed their way?
   Does anyone remember
   The words you spoke today?
   When the day is almost over
   And its toiling time is through,
   Will there be anyone to utter
      A friendly word for you?

Can you say tonight in passing,
   With the day that slipped so fast,
   That you helped a single person
   Of the many that you passed?
   Is a single heart rejoicing
   Over what you did or said?
   Does one whose hopes were fading
      Now with courage look ahead?

Did you waste the day or lose it?
   Was it well or poorly spent?
   Did you leave a trail of kindness
      Or a scar of discontent?

(Author Unknown)

"*I am only one, but I am one. That which I can do, I ought to do. That which I ought to do, by the grace of God, I will do.*"

- Everett Hale

Finding Peace, Purpose, and Happiness

*H*aving had the opportunity as a high school teacher and coach to closely observe communities, families, and young people for almost a half century, I've seen good times and bad times. *The Power of Becoming* was written to reflect on what has been observed and to offer some suggestions about those insights.

The bottom line of living is that all of mankind wants to "become something." I believe we want to love and be loved, want to be challenged, and want to have ownership. I also think deep inside all of us we each want to have a philosophy of life. If we satisfy these four wishes, we feel fulfilled. We feel like we have "become something." *The Power of Becoming* is a book about **becoming** the best that we can be.

Power. Brute power, brain power, electric power, nuclear power, "Paw Power," Almighty power, God power. All kinds of power. *The Power of Becoming*. This book is about taking the physical, intellectual, and spiritual powers that each of us has been given and using those powers to the maximum. Many of us have hidden gifts that we haven't even tapped. *The Power of Becoming* will help us to discover them if we are receptive. Uncovering latent power and using more wisely the talents we have will enable us to daily live more happily and purposefully. It is often a confusing, complex modern world. However, no matter what the challenges are, becoming the very best that we can be will help us find peace and satisfaction in our lives.

How do we do it? To begin with, Socrates, the great Greek philosopher, put it simply, "Know Thyself." Being honest about who you are, what you are, and what you are becoming in the grand scheme of things is part of this book's purpose. That is **becoming**. In William Shakespeare's classic drama *Hamlet*, a father advises his son, "To thine own self be true, and it must follow, as the night the day, thou canst not then be false to any man (Act I, sc. 3, l.78-80)." That is becoming.

Being true to yourself. What does that mean to actor Morgan Freeman? In a televised interview, he spoke of the ordeal of finding the best occupation for his life and abilities. What would give real purpose, peace, and happiness to living? Finally, after many years of searching, Freeman "found himself" in acting. He tapped the power of becoming and became the ultimate Morgan Freeman.

Most people struggle with such choices because they are afraid to take inventory of themselves and to pursue realistic dreams based on their findings. Oh yes, they are occasionally happy. They, at times, feel partial fulfillment of their hopes. However, more often than not, they feel incomplete and dissatisfied. They are afraid to dream because their dreams might not come true. Quite simply, mankind has be-come afraid to fail. Joe Paterno, the legendary Penn State football coach, puts it this way, "If you are afraid of losing, you will never win." Fear causes people to often settle for meaningless jobs, frivolous entertainment, and uninspired living. Morgan Freeman wasn't afraid to dream. This book is about your and my hopes and dreams. This book is about becoming the "whole package." It is about becoming the people we were really meant to be.

I take to heart Stephen Grellet's moving sentiments in "The Wayfarers."

> *"I expect to pass through this world but once;*
> *Any good thing therefore that I can do,*
> *Or any kindness that I can show to any fellow-creature,*
> *Let me do it now;*
> *Let me not defer or neglect it,*
> *For I shall not pass this way again."*

In 1960, celebrated American author John Steinbeck packed up his pickup truck and decided to rediscover his country. He traveled coast-to-coast with his French poodle, Charley, his only companion. Steinbeck published his account as *Travels With Charley*. Newsman Charles Kuralt made a thirty year livelihood traveling and chronicling America on network television. After retiring from CBS in 1994, he decided to do a sayonara of his favorite places in their favorite seasons. The result was a book entitled *Charles Kuralt's America*. How about if we take inventory of ourselves and do some traveling of our own? We are, after all, John Bunyan's modern day "Pilgrims," aren't we? Let's call our journeying *The Power of Becoming*.

The *Power of Becoming* will help us achieve the peace, purpose, and happiness of the life we desire by exploring several questions: As a traveler through this world, just who am I anyway? Who are these others? Where am I? What are we doing here? Where am I going? Why am I here, doing what I am doing? Whatever I am doing, how can I do it better? How do I interact with these others who also walk the highways of life with me?

The book's introductory poem "Consider" implies that we **become** when we care about more than ourselves. When we care and help other travelers on life's roads, we become what we were meant to be: fellowmen, brothers, soul mates. The ultimate participation in living is caring, helping, and giving. Acts of sharing are really acts of love. Loving and being loved are basic instincts. By sharing ourselves, our time, and our possessions, we become our natural best. A life with love is as good as life gets!

Nevertheless, despite the simplicity of the above prescription for successful living, our modern world often demonstrates the very opposite of caring and sharing. We often are greedy and tend to live only for ourselves. As Paterno said, we tend to live in fear. Are we becoming what man was meant to be in those instances?

> What is man that you are mindful of him,
> the son of man that you care for him?
> You made him a little lower than the angels;
> You crowned him with glory and honor
> And put everything under his feet.
> In putting everything under him,
> God left nothing that is not subject to him.
> Yet at present we do not see everything subject to him.
>
> (Hebrews 2:6-8 NIV)

What is man? I firmly believe that mankind must become more than assaulting, assaulted, terrorizing, and terrorized humanity. We must become more than money-hogging, chest-bumping, win-at-all-costs, take-the-Christ-out-of-Christmas creatures. We are surely more than Roy Andrew's "apes with possibilities" or Fulton Sheen's "jokers in the deck of nature," aren't we? Phillip Wylie describes mankind as "the organ of the accumulated smut and sneakery of 10,000 generations of weaseling souls." Apes, jokers, weaseling souls. Oh my, our travels are surely going to be challenging if any of these definitions are true.

In relationship to time itself, you and I must admit we are short-term travelers. As Isaac Watts wrote, "Time like an ever-rolling stream bears all its sons away." We are limited by our life expectancies, abilities, culture, and our opportunities. We need to get "worldly wise" fast. Paving a smoother road for ourselves and others will give our efforts enduring worthiness, even if our lives themselves are relatively brief. As Edward Everett Hale put it, "I am only one, but I am one. That which I can do, I ought to do. That which I ought to do, by the grace of God, I will do."

Newscaster Tom Brokaw wrote *The Greatest Generation,* a book about the men and women who fought World War II for us. They sacrificed lives and limbs for the freedoms we enjoy today. Their new and better understanding of the world expanded human rights, women's rights and civil rights. We can become a "great generation" too. We become people at our best when we give our spiritual support, intellectual know-how, and physical energy to our fellowmen.

Great generations achieve personal fulfillment and greatness in **becoming**. The following chapter outline is the basic format of the book built around the motif word, *Becoming:*

Chapter 1 **Becoming** is the Most Important Word in the World
Chapter 2 Real Power People Worth **Becoming**
Chapter 3 **Becoming** Real...Like a Child
Chapter 4 **Becoming** Three-Dimensional
Chapter 5 **Becoming** a Believer
Chapter 6 To Love and Be Loved
Chapter 7 To Work Is To **Become**
Chapter 8 What Work?
Chapter 9 Little Things Mean A Lot
Chapter 10 Calm After "The Sky Is Falling" Night!
Chapter 11 Having Fun, Fun, Fun While **Becoming**

Complementing the above chapters are practical, how-to essays: We Are "Part of the Main," Four Things a Man Must Learn To Do, Love Is An Enigma, and There Shall Be No More Death. Interspersed among the chapters and essays are letters to people you and I en-counter in our travels: Dear Young People, Dearly Beloved Wife or Husband, Dear Custodial Engineer, Dear Boss, or Dear Golden Ager. Obviously, you can read them in whatever order you please. Select the chapter, essay, or letter that fits your needs at a particular time in your life. I believe that you will enjoy both the variety of literary forms and the potpourri of literary selections.

Finally, we must remember to wisely use the time we have been given. We aren't immortal yet! Let's consider who we are, where we have been so far, what we are doing now, and where we are going. Let's also recognize our fellow wayfarers. They are kindred travel compan-ions. If we do these things, then it will be a worthwhile trip. We will indeed have begun to "**become something.**"

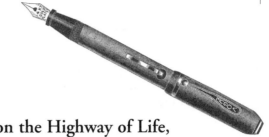

Today, AD
Truckstop, World

Dear Fellow Traveler on the Highway of Life,

Some wise man said, "If life is a journey, then we all are travelers." Well, then, all right. In my opinion, traveling alone isn't all that much fun anyway.

I say to you then today, "Hi! How ya' doin'? Good? OK? Sometimes not so hot? I know what you mean. Same thing over here."

A volume of Edgar Guest's poetry is entitled *A Heap O' Livin' Along Life's Highway*. When I finish traveling some day, I hope people will say of me, "He did a heap o' livin'!" How about you?

Fellow traveler, how's your "livin' " these days? I'm curious about you, as well as about me, our journey, and our fellowship. That said, where have you been so far? Nowhere much? Only around home? Several states? All fifty? World-wide? Wow! It really doesn't matter where we've been though, does it? Travel is travel, one place or another. We both can appreciate that. We're both trying to make our way down the road of life to somewhere. The color of the traveler's skin really doesn't matter. Size of body or brain doesn't matter either. Are you pretty...scarred...brave...scared? It doesn't matter. We're fellow travelers on the road of life. "We." Just respect the "We." In the ruts of a path, on a weaving trail, gravel or tar or concrete, two lane or six lanes...it doesn't matter. Just respect the "We," fellow traveler.

In my opinion, never has the world needed respect more than today. Simple mutual respect will make our travels smoother and safer. Yet we're not only travelers. We're also gladiators of a sort. Our journey is also a rite of passage, a test, an ordeal. All of us—pilgrims, gladiators, travelers—strive, stumble, and fall. That is a natural part of traveling.

Do you know where you are going? I'm not positive where I'm headed. I'd like to be sure. George Moore in *The Brook Karuth* writes, " A man travels the world in search of what he needs and returns home to find it." Is that the same as "home is where the heart is"? Is this why a 92-year-old aunt moving from home to hospital to care center declared, "All I want to do is go home"? However, the hymn "I'm But a Stranger Here" exclaims otherwise: "Heaven is my home."

What are you and I searching for among the side roads, byroads, detours, high roads, and low roads that we travel? Robert Frost's poem, "The Road Not Taken" says that "two roads diverged in a woods, and I took the one less traveled by, and that has made all the difference." Perhaps "making a difference" is the difference.

I hope you and I can make a difference in others' lives by recognizing each other as fellow travelers, as "A being breathing thoughtful breath; a traveler betwixt life and death," in the words of William Wordsworth. More amusingly, I also admire Harry Woods' lyrics from his song "Side by Side."

> "Oh, we ain't got a barrel of money,
> Maybe we're ragged and funny,
> But we'll travel along
> Singing a song,
> Side by side."

(Humming, whistling, or lip synching works too!)

When we meet again, fellow traveler, I want to reach out and firmly shake your hand. Let's be strong in our "hellos" and in our "good-byes." Let's be strong in our travels. Please reach out and shake hands meaningfully. If we become strong together, regardless of race, creed, politics, or culture, we will travel life's highways well. Let's **Become** strong.

Sincerely,

A Fellow Traveler

We Are "Part of the Main"

Who are we anyway? We have been suggesting that we all are way-farers or travelers on the super highways of life. Travelers...there are a lot of us: 6,492,665,129 at my last check of references.

The Indispensable Man

Sometime, when you're feeling important
Sometime, when your ego's in bloom,
Sometime, when you take it for granted,
You're the best qualified in the room.
Sometime, when you feel your going,
Would leave an unfillable hole,
Just follow this simple instruction,
And see how it humbles your soul.

Take a bucket and fill it with water;
Put your hand in it, up to the wrist;
Pull it out, and the hole that's remaining,
Is a measure of how you'll be missed.

You may splash all you please when you enter,
You can stir up the water galore;
But stop and you'll find in a minute,
That it looks quite the same as before.
The moral in this quaint example,
Is to do just the best that you can.
Be proud of yourself, but remember,
There's no indispensable man!!!

- Anonymous

It is like being a grain of sand on a never ending seashore of humanity. As such, we must recognize that we're pretty microscopic in the big picture. We are definitely not indispensable. When we are gone, there will be another one to replace us travelers, grains of sand, or "whatevers." However, as Edward Everett Hale was quoted in the Prologue, "I am only one, but I am one." I do count too. Above all, "I am."

Nevertheless, we are still parts of the whole. We are pieces of the puzzle of life. We have significance in our eras. If we can discover "Who we are," we will have purpose. Knowing who we are will enable us to better determine where we should travel. With purpose we need not be overwhelmed by the billions of others on the seashore nor by the miles of landscape. However, be humble. Even though we know who we are, we can be replaced. We are all but grains of sand on the seashore of life. As John Donne says in *Meditation 17*:

> "No man is an island entire of itself,
> every man is a piece of the
> Continent, a part of the main."

Despite the numbers game being very humbling, our individuality is still very important. The seashore began with a grain of sand. Log cabins began with one log. Foundations are begun with one brick. Skyscrapers start with one girder. I am one. One is important. Which one am I? Who really am I? Remember the axiom, "I had no shoes and I complained until I met a man who had no feet"? Or the blind man who daily sold shoe laces in an eastern city? Shabby, beater coat, smoked glasses, and a white cane. Around his neck hung a small metal plate on which was engraved, "It could be worse." Be thankful and humble for whoever and whatever you are. Go as far as you can, as long as you can, with what you have. That is enough. The people mentioned above and you and I all began in the same way as those illustrated in the following paragraph, single pebbles on the seashore of life.

Inside a hospital nursery, eight well-wrapped newborns in pink and blue are drawing their first impressions of the outside world. In reality, several are blissfully sleeping, having surmised that this is a "good" place, just like the one they recently left. The heads of a couple of the others are wobbling up and down, skeptical of this new environment. Here and there, a nursling starts to fuss, perhaps about the food supply, and another one actually begins to cry, uncertain of the whole situation. For the next couple days, the loving, adoring, curious, smiling, proud faces of parents, families, and friends will take their shifts admiring the infants and extolling their various virtues. "Birth" day. The environments of our births themselves varied, but the emotions and reactions were similar. Who we are and what we are going to become began on that day.

The excitement and hubbub of hospital maternity wards and their nurseries is certainly one of the premier experiences of life. Being associated with that new baby is indeed gratifying, isn't it? Arrived from where? Going where? What a momentous day! A high of life! Weddings, graduations, reunions, and anniversaries bring some measure of the same exhilaration. Beginnings, premier experiences of life, moments of sheer ecstasy.

The exact opposite polarity of emotion was also sensed recently while attending the funeral of a teenager, sharing in the tearful grieving of family and friends, and trying to draw meaning from life's sudden exits. Anxiety, sorrow, and anguish were everywhere. Why? Why? Why? Accidents, natural disasters, hospitalization, and, of course, war are other examples of these confusing, heart-rending intrusions, stoppages and, sometimes, exits from life. Let's not be naïve. No matter who we are, all will exit as well as enter life. Keep in mind Stephen Grellet's verse from the Prologue: "I expect to pass through this world but once." Exodus, isolation, parting...life's moments of sheer agony, indelibly dramatic experiences too.

Having considered the above, we might conclude that it would be healthful for every person on earth to go to a hospital nursery, a wedding ceremony, a hospital intensive care unit, a chemo treatment center, and a funeral periodically, at least once a year. Perhaps we could include in our dream world itinerary a visit to other countries with different cultural and social appreciations than ours. A walk through a farmer's field at harvest time, another walk across the front lines at a war front, and a third walk up a mountain trail alongside a trout stream would all be worth the effort for every human being. Finally, let us all visit an inner city ghetto, the cells of an over-populated prison, and an Alzheimer's wing at a care center for the elderly.

Why should we do these things? Simply to learn first hand about who we are, who those others are, and what fundamentally our lives involve. From the date of birth, we are most certainly here. We come and go. Fate may determine our times and places. Is there more? Why not attempt to understand the significance of who we are, and what the world is all about? Who are these "companions" on this planet, where are we travelers all going, and what are we masses all doing here anyway? The answers should help us appreciate, gain perspective, and grow in understanding as to what life is all about. If all of us could experience these situations periodically, Harold Chapin's song lyrics would more than echo, "This world would be a better place...for you...for me." I maintain we'd respect more, love more, and, conversely, dislike less, hate less, and ultimately war less. Who are we? Answer it honestly. Live according to your answer.

"Who are we? Who are we? Who are we?" This haunting refrain was a recurring question running through an educational film entitled, "The Humanities: A Search for Meaning." The film depicts mankind's efforts to find identity and to live meaningfully through art, music, literature, science, technology, work, and play throughout the ages. It is a kaleidoscope of images from space travel to Picasso to Mozart to skyscrapers to cancer research to children swinging on playground equipment to both literal and figurative cops and robbers. The question is universal. The question is eternal. "Who are we?" or "Who am I?" "What am I? What am I doing? Why am I doing it? Who are these others? Where are we going? Why?"

Arthur Miller's classic drama, *Death of a Salesman*, poignantly speaks to the importance of answering this question of "Who are we?" Biff, the son of the lead character Willy Loman, says of his father at the end of the play, "He had the wrong dreams. He never knew who he was." Willy, you, me...we all are "Someone." We all have an identity. We all have an identifying story that needs to be heard. Willy mournfully laments late in the drama, "I'm not a dime a dozen!" His life had belied this. You were right, Willy: "GDMNJ: God Don't Make No Junk."

"Who are we? Really, who are we?" We need to have answers to these questions before any of the other pieces of the puzzle slip into place. Life needs meaning. Life needs purpose. Otherwise, truly, why get up in the morning? It seems to me that without meaning and purpose, I am no more than an animal. I live to eat, breed, sleep . . . . eat, breed, sleep. Isn't man more than that? "What 'cha doing?" "Nothing." "Where ya going?" "Nowhere." "Come on along." Maybe it's "Let's go fast." Fast cars, fast friends, fast sex, fast chemicals, fast games. Maybe it's "Let's go slow." Sleep the day away, smoke the day away, eat the day away, couch potato the day away. Whatever, "Come on along."

Who am I? Doctors, lawyers, educators, athletes, entertainers, truck drivers, secretaries, manual laborers: we all have our stories. Am I a passive, apathetic, "the-world-must-come-to-me," non-participant in life? Or am I an active, caring, "I want to be involved" participant in life? Do I love living? Let's make our story an analogous, rural example. Am I the farmer who sits on a stool in the middle of the pasture waiting for the cow to back up to him for milking? Or am I the man who takes pride in his herd, calls each cow by name, and feeds, pets, and milks each animal with the utmost love? Is my existence merely inhaling, exhaling, and sitting in a pasture literally watching the grass grow? If so, it is too meager.

Who am I? A member of mankind, not indispensable. One human out of 6,492,665,129 (and counting) members of that human race

(US Census Bureau, 9/21/05). "Every man is a piece of the Continent, a part of the Main." Not more, nor less, but just as important a piece of the continent as anyone else. A participant in life from crib to coffin. Sensitive to personal ups and downs. Hopefully, empathetic to the ups and downs of others. I'm not a dime a dozen. I do need to understand myself in order to have meaning and purpose to my days. Socrates advises each of us to "Know Thyself." If we know, we can **Become**. Maybe even become footprints on the sands of time. Obviously, it is only a figure of speech, but maybe we can become farmers who love and care, who are not just "milkers" of life, only taking and not giving back. Whatever field of work you choose, do it wholeheartedly. Give it love. To do any of this, however, we must begin by knowing "Who We Are." Unquestionably, we are "part of the Main."

" *I* have no yesterday. Time took them away.
Tomorrow may not be. But I have today. "

- Pearl Yeadon McGinnis

CHAPTER ONE

Becoming Is the Most Important Word in the World!

"All right, give me the single, most important word in the world. The word needs to exude the potential of power. You can only choose one though."

"Only one? Come on. You gotta' be kidding! A zillion important words and oodles of powerful ones!"

*　　*　　*　　*　　*　　*

All right, let's throw away our dictionaries and thesauruses. Let's simply try looking inside ourselves for the one most important word. Do you really want to be "Captain of your ship, Master of your fate?" Do you really want the power to call the shots? Then, call on the force from within, the drive to become. The ultimate word is **Becoming**.

Inside every human being is the ability to become. What are you becoming right now, at this very moment? In her poem "Today," Pearl Yeadon McGinnis writes, "I have no yesterday. Time took them away. Tomorrow may not be. But I have today." What are you becoming? Change occurs every moment of our existence. Are you changing for better or worse? This book is about you and me becoming the best people we can be. People who find meaning in their daily living. People who appreciate their fellowmen and can live peaceably with them. People who are positive in their outlooks on life and who basically live in the pursuit of happiness. Wouldn't you like to become one of them?

These days I am a husband, a relative, and a friend. I find myself writing, coaching, fathering, and grandfathering. In the past I have been a teacher, a colleague, a teammate, an acquaintance, and a son. How I performed in those areas in 1945, 1965, or 1985 isn't as important as how I perform them today. Someone protests, "Yes, but you were good at them!" Yesterday's headlines! Another voice, mine, apologetically chimes in, "Yeah, well, the real truth was I never was exceptionally good at any of them." Again, who cares? Old news. It's history! The only important thing is what are we becoming today.

Your past doesn't matter. That's history. What are you today? What are you becoming? A greater or poorer shingle-layer, garbage man, nurse's aide, secretary, sales clerk, custodian, reserve on the high school team, captain of the team, class vice-president, vice president of a small company, newscaster, news reporter, shipping clerk, assembly line worker at 3M, General Motors CEO, bartender, waitress, convict, policeman, fireman, Secretary-General of the United Nations, etc.? Today? Greater or poorer?

Building

For Yesterday is but a Dream,
And Tomorrow is only a Vision;
But Today, well-lived,
Makes every Yesterday
A Dream of Happiness,
And every Tomorrow a Vision of Hope.

(Author Unknown)

John Donne, the great English metaphysical poet said, "What if this present evening were the world's last night?" One year, one month, one week to live would make many of us into philosophers, wouldn't it? Assuredly, a lot of the human race would be scrambling "if this present evening were the world's last night." A sad irony of our own species is that wisdom often comes with age and experience. And man dies! How unfortunate that appreciation of our really having physical, intellectual, and spiritual dimensions comes to many people so late in life. Why wait until middle age or later to watch what you eat and to exercise? Why wait until then to appreciate classical music, books, or art? Why wait until the Golden Years to look for answers in the longest lasting, and most widely sold book in history, the *Bible*? Terminal illness and military service, emphysema and the Grim Reaper, Alzheimer's and loss of memory, and broken spirits and the prospect of a Judgment Day shake the minds of people of all ages.

H. W. Longfellow tells us, "We can make our lives sublime and departing, leave behind us footprints in the sands of time." What are your footprints becoming?

THE PAST

Learn from the past.

Time occupies a central place in many of Shakespeare's works. King Macbeth expresses his pessimism about time in Act V of *Macbeth*. His wife has died, and he says:

> Tomorrow, and tomorrow, and tomorrow,
> Creeps in this petty pace from day to day
> To the last syllable of recorded time;
> And all our yesterdays have lighted fools
> The way to dusty death. Out, out, brief candle!
> Life's but a walking shadow, a poor player,
> That struts and frets his hour upon the stage,

And then is heard no more; it is a tale

Told by an idiot, full of sound and fury, signifying nothing.

Henry Dobson, in his poem "The Paradox of Time" notes, "Time goes, you say? Ah, no! Alas, time stays, we go." George Peale tells us, "His golden locks time hath to silver turned; O time too swift, O swiftness never ceasing!" For years a slogan appeared by my classroom clock, "Time passes. Will you?" Will we pass the test of time? "All our yesterdays have lighted fools the way to dusty death." Unquestionably, Macbeth, we can't stop time nor death. However, fools we need not be!

Experiences can help us become better in the present. Learn from them. Use them. Assuredly, don't ignore them. In *Richard II*, Shakespeare uses time again: "I wasted time and now time doth waste me." Don't waste it. As a teacher, coach, husband, and parent, I certainly make mistakes. I speak too quickly, I hurt feelings, and I overlook opportunities. As I mature, I find that if I don't waste time, then such things happen less often. I become better.

Similarly, my past successes enliven my present-day experiences and attitudes. "Moments to Remember," a nostalgic song by the Four Lads, speaks of "quiet walks, the noisy fun, the ballroom prize we almost won." Today's successes may be as simple as appreciation for the everyday experiences we all have. It could be fresh air, a soothing bath or shower, or the "Big One" that got away. It might simply be our thanking or praising coworkers, acquaintances, family, students, athletes, whomever. Respect, gratitude, and praise are success stories in miniature. It's a Win-Win situation. Use the past to learn from, both the failures and successes. Becoming.

THE PRESENT

Use the present. *Carpe diem,* "Seize the day." Make hay while the sun shines. Bloom where you are planted. Such expressions remind us to use our time wisely. On my desk for years has been a coaster that I especially have appreciated which reads "Bloom where planted." We spend too much time dreaming of "the good old days," of the "greener grass across the road," or of "the pie in the sky in the near by and by," and we never bloom. Remember the poem, "Consider," that opened this book? As the poet suggested, never, if possible, lie down at night without being able to say, "I have made one human being, at least, a little wiser, a little happier, or a little better this day." That's "Seizing the day." Becoming.

A. E. Housman, in his poem "A Shropshire Lad" writes

> Clay lies still, but blood's a rover,
> Breath's a ware that will not keep,
> Up, lad, when the journey's over,
> There'll be time enough to sleep.

Time

Take time to pray...it helps to bring God near and
washes the dust of earth from your eyes.
Take time for friends...it is the source of happiness.
Take time for work...it is the price of success.
Take time to think...it is the source of power.
Take time to read...it is the foundation of knowledge.
Take time to laugh...it is the singing that helps with life's road.
Take time to love...it is the one sacrament of life.
Take time to dream...it hitches the soul to the stars.
Take time to play...it is the secret of youth.
Take time to worship...it is the highway to reverence.

- Author Unknown

To become is to use the present moment to the fullest. To become is to follow Charles Kingsley's advice to "make a fellow human wiser, happier, or better for crossing paths with you this day." That's worthwhile. That's becoming.

THE FUTURE

Look to the horizon. The future is the result of what we learn from our past and how we use the present. As we become, our future becomes rewarding. Believe. Be bold. Become.

Our goals need to be grand, yet attainable. Aim high. Even if you land short, you've still traveled and achieved. Reverend Robert Schuller makes the point vividly: "Inch by inch, everything's a cinch. Yard by yard, everything is hard."

Ralph Waldo Emerson expresses this sense of forward momentum in "One Day at a Time."

"Finish every day and be done with it. You have done what you could. Some blunders and absurdities no doubt crept in; forget them as soon as you can. Tomorrow is a new day; begin it well and serenely and with too high a spirit to be cumbered with your old nonsense. This day is all that's good and fair. It is too dear, with its hopes and invitations, to waste a moment on yesterdays."

I enjoy the metaphor of blank paper or a clean slate. I imagine that life is a tablet of clean, white paper. Each day we get a new sheet. We can scrawl or inscribe. We can dabble or paint. We can blot or blemish. Create messes or masterpieces. Tomorrow, we will have a new, clean page upon which to leave our mark again. Each of us writes a book of life. Become all you can be.

*J*ust For Today

Just for today, I will try to live through this
day only, and not tackle my whole life problem
at once. I can do something for twelve hours
that would appall me if I felt that I had to
keep it up for a lifetime.

Just for today, I will be happy. This assumes to
be true what Abraham Lincoln said, that
"most folks are as happy as they make up
their minds to be."

Just for today, I will try to strengthen my mind.
I will study. I will learn something useful.
I will not be a mental loafer. I will read
something that requires effort, thought and
concentration.

Just for today, I will adjust myself to what is,
and not try to adjust everything to my own
desires. I will take my "luck" as it comes,
and fit myself to it.

Just for today, I will exercise my soul in three
ways: I will do somebody a good turn, and
not get found out. I will do at least two
things I don't want to do...just for exercise.
I will not show anyone that my feelings are
hurt; they may be hurt, but today I will not show it.

Just for today, I will be agreeable. I will look
as well as I can, dress becomingly, talk low,
act courteously, criticize not one bit, not
find fault with anything and not try to
improve or regulate anybody except myself.
Just for today, I will have a program. I may not
follow it exactly, but I will have it. I will
save myself from two pests: hurry and indecision.

Just for today, I will have a quiet half hour all
by myself, and relax. During this half hour,
sometime, I will try to get a better perspective
of my life.

Just for today, I will be unafraid. Especially I
will not be afraid to enjoy what is beautiful,
and to believe that as I give to the world, so
the world will give to me.

- Kenneth Holmes

I like the acronym "K.I.S.S." That is "Keep It Simple, Solomon (not the traditional *S*= Stupid)." This implies to me, "Keep it simple as you pursue *The Power of Becoming*. Keep it simple as you grow in wisdom and truth." Simplify it to one word, **Becoming**. Reduce. Simplify. Henry Thoreau did this when he moved his entire existence to Walden Pond in order to live simply and commune with nature and nothing else. For him, this life became the ultimate good life. The most important word in the world, Solomon? **Becoming!** *The Power of Becoming*!

*"There is no **I** in **TEAM**."*

CHAPTER TWO

Real Power People Worth Becoming

Who are we? Do we really know ourselves? Some of us are concealing our true identity. We're often in disguise. Why? Let's take off our masks! Who will we see then? Real people, that's who. To be real takes strength of character. Let's become real.

Who am I? Who are you? Who are we? To find out more about ourselves, we can actually study and learn from others. Every one of us has a story worth hearing. Let's explore some heroic examples of up-front, no mask, what-you-see-is-what-you-get, honest people. Real people. Take time to study people who have qualities we might emulate. It will help us to be more open about ourselves. The people below are doing or have done a lot of things right. They had or have reasons to get up in the morning. They represent the power of becoming. Let's join them. Ready?

LANCE ARMSTRONG

Lance Armstrong won the tortuous Tour de France bicycle road race for the seventh consecutive time in 2005. This challenge involves 21 days of racing, 3630 kilometers of roadways, and 3 mountaintop finishes. In 1997 Lance was diagnosed with life-threatening testicular cancer, which ultimately spread to his lungs and brain. He endured. He responded to challenge. His leadership in the fight against cancer is an inspiration to all today. Lance conquered the disease and the road again. He beat cancer and competing cyclists. Great ones respond when challenged. Are we responding to our challenges?

THE FOSS FAMILY

The Foss family inspires me. They exemplify loving perseverance. Each week I see Don Foss, his sons Eric and Dan, and Don's wife Carrie en route to church. Carrie helps each from the van into his own wheelchair. This regular ritual in sun, rain, or snow was loving perseverance at its ultimate. Don fought through triple-bypass heart surgery, a kidney transplant, and debilitating medicinal side-effects before passing away recently. Eric and Dan both are in life-long struggles with polyarteritis. Dan also endured a kidney transplant. This family humbles all of us in their perseverance, patience, faithfulness, and reverence. Are we persevering?

BILL MCCARTNEY

Bill McCartney was the very successful head football coach of the University of Colorado Buffaloes. He felt a call, kept the promise of that call, and is humbly and steadfastly pursuing that dream. The great ones have initiative and are enterprising, and not merely about offensive formations or defensive stunts. Coach McCartney left the limelight of big-time collegiate football for relative obscurity as the founding father of The Promise Keepers. This international organization is dedicated to men living up to their biblical callings to fulfill their "promise" as male role models in the world. Over five million men have participated in The Promise Keepers' 100-plus conferences in major stadiums and arenas since 1990. The title of his 1997 book,

Sold Out: Becoming Man Enough To Make a Difference, could symbolize his decision to leave the world of fleeting glory to pursue the world of lasting glory. Yet the book focuses on the inherent didactic challenge for anyone seeking to make a difference. Are we keeping our promises and living up to our promise?

VERONICA PASLAWSKI

Veronica Paslawski plays in a summer-long six-to-eight-year-old boys and girls baseball program. Veronica smiles as she gets out of the car and makes her way to the field. It's a great smile. It would be great with or without her physical handicap.

Down syndrome or not, no one runs to a defensive position as intently as she does. No one hustles as enthusiastically back to the bench to wait a turn to bat. Veronica is all-star material because she always gives her best. Heads-of-State, nuclear physicists, professional athletes, entertainers, small business operators, parents, peers...all should try as hard as she does.

If coaches show how to throw the ball with the fingers across the seams, Veronica grips the ball across the seams. If a fielding glove is supposed to be up for one type of catch, but turned down for another type, rest assured she will try to do it the right way. Everyone should be so coachable, so eager to learn and try.

I most admire Veronica when she is batting. No one is more determined at bat. I watch her cock her head to a 45-degree angle to better see the pitcher through her glasses. Her cap seems precariously tilted, but it doesn't fall off as she takes her best swings. She's a "swinger," not a "taker," a doer, not a watcher. Her demeanor makes me want to cheer before, during, and after her at-bats. After she hits, I wish the fielders nothing but bad luck as she heads for first base. There is no one among our 600 players that I'm happier to see leg out a grounder and reach base. I'm not the only one cheering.

Listen to them, Veronica. Listen and smile. No one deserves those cheers more than you.

Invariably, practice or games, Veronica seeks out her leader before heading home. Each time, she offers the same enthusiastic "Thank you, Coach." Her words are heartfelt and sincere.

Your thoughtfulness, diligence, hustle, and effort are exemplary, little lady. Are we anywhere near the standards Veronica sets?

DAVE NELSON

In three years Dave Nelson brought a suburban high school in Minnetonka, Minnesota, from relative obscurity and a 1-8 record to a state football championship. I coached for a number of years against him at his original teaching and coaching position at Blaine High School where he served for 23 years, 18 as head football coach. I had the opportunity to assist him there after my retirement from teaching. Blaine's record was 0-8 when he took over.

In 2004 Minnetonka made its first state tournament appearance. Blaine made it eight times, appeared in the championship game four times, and won it all once. Dave Nelson was always hard to beat, on the field as a coach or off the field as a human being. Several characteristics make Dave exemplary.

"There is no *I* in Team."

Players, coaches, coaches' families and loved ones, parents, faculty, and fans are all part of Dave's team. All work together, study together, share together, cheer together, and socialize together. Yet they do so without suffocating each other. All are pieces of the same puzzle. Everyone can count on each other. All are treated with respect.

Self-Sacrifice

I've seen him leave school at 6:30 p.m. to go home and spend several hours of quality time with his wife, daughters, and son, only to return to school for late-evening hours of study and work. His home has sacrificed to take in athletes who are in disadvantaged domestic situations. Certainly the hours spent in developing good public relations with the community are another example of sacrifice. After the recent state semi-final game, Coach Nelson urged his players to do community service the next morning. Self-sacrifice is love. Thankfully it is contagious.

Life's Tangible Rewards

Weight room accomplishments by football players may be acknowledged on an eye-catching bulletin board. They may be acknowledged through the awarding of tee-shirts. Shirts might also be presented to the best "Scout Team Offensive and Defensive Player of the Week," best "Junior Varsity Player of the Week," as well as normal varsity game awards. These are valuable incentives for a team.

The secretaries, custodians, and go-fers in your business or organization are just as important to your "team" as the CEOs. Reward them in some noteworthy ways too.

Ambiance

On a bright well-painted board hanging in the coaches' offices is a well-grounded biblical principle of teaching: "Be prepared in season and out of season; correct, rebuke, and encourage...with great patience and careful instruction" (II Timothy 4:2 NIV). Coaches see it daily before they begin their work. There are large, eye-catching plaque boards hanging in the locker room saluting "Team Pride," "Best Defense Efforts," and "Biggest Comebacks" throughout history. As you enter the gate to the practice fields, a final admonition catches your eye: "Do It Right. Do It Hard. Or, Do It Again." A healthy pride is fostered everywhere.

Thoughtfulness

Dave reaches out to the hurting, the less gifted, the ones performing menial tasks, as well as to those who are more visible. He cares about players, a staff member's family, and his business acquaintances. He cares about his own father and mother, his roots. Invariably, on game night Dave leaves the team's pre-game warm-up to walk to the field's restraining fence to give a hug and a hand shake to his parents. He gives. He cares. Do we?

CHARISMATIC

We can learn from animals too. The 1999 Kentucky Derby winner, Charismatic, has one of the all-time great names. Charisma: "personal magnetism and charm." Put a warm-hearted, enthusiastic personality with a friendly, smiling face and you have charisma plus. I want that.

Do you know that rare individual who perpetually radiates, even as he or she is conducting business? Kids have it naturally. I recall one of our children sitting in a high chair, slurping an orange popsicle, and munching wads of birthday cake. This orgy is punctuated with smiles that would guarantee world peace. Oh, the unsurpassed, irrepressible innocence and enthusiasm of a child!

Have you known people it is just a pleasure to listen to, to learn from, and to follow? Charisma. Leadership. Persona. Have you felt a room lighten or a mood brighten from the smile of someone you respect and admire? Smiles and charisma. Truly, one of the earth's great pleasures is to be in the company of charming, magnetic people. Do we radiate?

MOTHER TERESA

Reverend Robert Schuller describes Mother Teresa as "Tiny but powerful. Humble, but dignified. Intense and incredibly energetic. After only a minute in her presence I was reminded anew that Jesus Christ is alive."

Mother Teresa's work for the dying in Calcutta, India, earned her the Nobel Peace Prize. At the time of her 1997 death, Mother Teresa had established approximately 500 mission homes around the world in 80 countries. She and her 3000 Missionaries of Charity serve and give hope to the poor and underprivileged. When once asked where she wanted to be buried, she replied, "I don't know. Wherever it happens, whenever Jesus comes to take me." The question was not material to the real things of life.

Mother Teresa distinguished between physical and emotional starvation.

I try to save people from dying because of physical starvation. In America, people are dying of emotional starvation. Emotional starvation is the hunger to be something to somebody. I've seen people suffering from physical starvation die beautifully. They die at peace with God. But a person who is lonely, unwanted, and uncared for, left alone like that, has a terrible bitterness that closes the heart to anybody and anything. They may commit suicide from this anger and frustration. It's more difficult in rich countries than in Africa or India. When I find someone starving, I can take him to my home and give him something to eat. I have removed his basic difficulty. If I keep him longer and put him on his feet, then it's finished. I'll never forget one day I met a man in the street in London and he looked so terrible. I went to him and I took his hand and the hand I held was very cold. Then he said, 'Oh, for a long, long time, I craved the warmth of a human hand.' And, he sat up and he gave me such a beautiful smile! But I don't know how many more times he's been alone now. This is what the people are hungry for...love.

I would like to bring prayer back into the lives of people, into all families, because love begins at home. And it begins by praying together. The family that prays together, always stays together, and they stay together united. They love one another, and they will never allow anything to break that unity and peace. It is very important that the families teach their children to pray and pray with them. We need a deep attachment to Christ. We have to be deeply, deeply prayerful and have a real deep love for prayer. We begin the day with meditation, Holy Mass with Holy Communion. And then we end the day with a full service of adoration, and that's something...the greatest gift of God to our society. I don't think I could do what I'm doing if I didn't have those four hours of prayer every day! Jesus said, 'Learn of me because I'm meek and humble of heart.' That's a beautiful thing. Dignity is learning to be meek and humble of heart and to be able to talk to God because God speaks in the silence of the heart and we listen. And then we speak to God from the fullness of our heart and he listens. That's prayer. And to be able to do that, we need a clean heart, for a clean heart can see God.

Keep on smiling, always. Keep on smiling because smiling is the beginning of peace. I have had a number of sisters who have not been able to smile with the people and be a cause of a joy to them. They found out it was not their vocation, and they have gone back home. Smiling is the best medicine for suffering, poverty, and dying. When you come with a smile, they feel loved and wanted. I thank God that I can laugh lots too, plenty at least.

Mother Teresa sets her standards heavenly high. Most of us can't be as saintly as Mother Teresa. However, are we at least humble?

The people above are real, no mask people. They are up-front and honest. They bloom wherever they happened to be. These men and women stand up for what they believe. Let's do as well. "Who am I? What-you-see-is-what-you-get. I am what I am. I'm real!" How does that sound to you? To be real is to be strong. Become the same.

" Every child comes with the message that God is not yet discouraged of man. "

- Rabindranath Tagore

CHAPTER THREE

Becoming Real...Like a Child!

*D*on't underestimate the importance of being childlike: innocent, unadorned, real. *Child*: kid, toddler, tyke, nipper, little shaver, munchkin, "an ever bubbling fountain in the world of humanity" (Friedrich Froebel). *Real*: actual, genuine, authentic, true, legitimate, bona fide.

One of our classic family pictures is that of a four-year old boy walking down the country driveway with his arm draped over the back of his dog, a 100 pound German Shepherd-Collie cross. A child with the child's best friend, his dog: *Real*. As time has rolled on, the boy above became a parent and then a grandparent: *Real*. Becoming the parents of one, two, three, four children, six grandchildren: *Real*, in retrospect! The innocence of those children being tickled and goosed by a lawn sprinkler; the smiles and squeals of those children at 4th of July fireworks exploding in the clear sky; the excitement of learning to read for the first time; the pleasure of riding a bike for the first time: *Real*. Childhood is special. To relive it through children and grandchildren is forever good. Don't be afraid to be real like a child. *Childlike*.

"Like or befitting a child, as in innocence." Discovering the real you and me is so critical to becoming our best selves. We are all winners when we are honest and open like a child.

William Blake, in his poem "Songs of Innocence," writes, "Piping down the valleys wild, Piping songs of pleasant glee, On a cloud I saw a child." The Bible asserts, "Suffer the little children to come onto me, and forbid them not; for of such is the kingdom of God" (Mark 10:14 NIV). Children and their childlike qualities are worth imitating for all of us, . The great American poet Carl Sandburg wrote "A baby is God's opinion that life should go on."

Listen also to the following anonymous poem drawn from The Treasure Chest, a Harper and Row album of inspirational cuttings collected in 1965.

A Little Child Shall Lead Us

You, little child, with your shining eyes and
dimpled cheeks, you can lead us along the
pathway to the more abundant life:
We blundering grownups need in our lives the
virtues that you have in yours:
the joy and enthusiasm of looking forward to
each new day with glorious expectations of
wonderful things to come.
The vision that sees the world as a splendid
place with good fairies, brave knights, and
glistening castles reaching toward the sky.
The radiant curiosity that finds adventure in
simple things: the mystery of billowy clouds,
the miracle of snowflakes,
the magic of growing flowers.
The tolerance that forgets differences as quickly

as your childish quarrels are spent, that holds no
grudges, that hates never, that loves people
for what they are.
The genuineness of being oneself; to be done
without sham, pretense, and empty show; to be
simple, natural, and sincere.
The courage that rises from defeat and tries
again, as you with laughing face rebuild the
house of blocks that topples to the floor.
The believing heart that trusts others, knows no
fear, and has faith in a Divine Father who
watches over his children from the sky.
The contented, trusting mind that at the close
of day woos the blessing of childlike slumber.
Little child, we would become like you, that we
may find again the Kingdom of Heaven
within our hearts.

Leo Tolstoy, in his epic novel *War and Peace*, uses effectively the motif of being childlike. An example is that of the young heroine Natasha's father speaking of "the eggs teaching the hen." The English poet William Wordsworth, in his poem, "My Heart Leaps Up When I Behold," writes that "The child is father of the man." Antoine de Saint-Exupery, in his classic *The Little Prince*, reminds us that "Grownups never understand anything for themselves, and it is tiresome for children to be always and forever explaining things to them." The American poet John Greenleaf Whittier writes:

> We need love's tender lessons taught
> As only weakness can;
> God hath his small interpreters;
> The child must teach the man.

In a similar vein Rabindranath Tagore tells us, "Every child comes with the message that God is not yet discouraged of man." I agree with the poets and sages: each little person is a fresh beginning of what mankind should really be like. *Real.*

Let's explore the desirable characteristics of children through an acronym. The examples are drawn from Tolstoy's *War and Peace.*

C - **Curious**

H - **Honest**

I - **Innocent**

L - **Loving**

D - **Dreamers**

R - **Receptive**

E - **Enthusiastic**

N - **Natural**

Curious

Natasha is in her early teens and is curious about the phenomenon of romantic love. The aristocratic Pierre Bezuhov is curious as to what war is really all about and naively wanders onto a battlefield in a suit and a hat. We learn by being curious. Hang onto curiosity.

Honest

"There was the same expression still on the charming childish face with the little lip covered with fine, dark hair. 'I love you all and have done no harm to anyone and what have you done to me?' said her charming, piteous dead face. Prince Andrey, her husband, sobbed like a child." Be honest in all of life before it is too late. Be real.

Innocent

Nicholas Rostov is a young soldier. He believes the battlefront holds only glory for the participant until his horse is shot out from under him, he's injured, and ultimately, he's pursued by French soldiers. In youthful panic, he throws his pistol at them! An even younger boy soldier, Petya Rostov, unwarily attempts to lead a guerrilla band of Cossacks on an ill-advised charge. He is shot and tumbles ingloriously into the smoldering ashes of a bonfire. Innocence, even in the heat of battle, describes us at our purest, most honest, and best. How can we retain this purity, yet not be destroyed by the world?

Loving

Andrey, returning to his boyhood home after the death of his first wife, finds a new, innocent, youthful love. It is love reincarnated. Pierre, finding real love with a young woman after being taken advantage of by an older woman, is a soul uplifted. What is more genuine than the love of a child? We adults need the innocence of love too. Be real, unaffected, and authentic.

Dreamers

Andrey sees hope for the future in a budding oak tree after a stark, sterile winter. Pierre foresees a meaningful future as he gazes at a comet. Who's better at hopes and dreams than a child? How about a 6-year old going to bed in his baseball T-shirt with his cap and glove by his side because Tee-ball begins in the morning? Are there any better dreams than that? Listen to Andrew Gillies in the following poem:

*T*wo Prayers

Last night my little boy confessed to me
Some childish wrong;
And kneeling at my knee,
He prayed with tears...
"Dear God, make me a man
Like Daddy...wise and strong;
I know you can."

Then while he slept
I knelt beside his bed,
Confessed my sins,
And prayed with low-bowed head...
"O God, make me a child
Like my child here...Pure, guileless,
Trusting Thee with faith sincere."

Receptive

Children, for the most part, are receptive to new ideas, new activities, new schedules. Adults are more reluctant. During the Napoleonic invasion, two competitors in love with the same woman both end up at the same time in the same first aid station with equally serious life-threatening wounds. Their rivalry through courtship is of no concern anymore. In life and death struggles, man is more readily receptive to the fact that we are all brothers. Let's retain our childhood receptiveness to "anything." Be open-minded.

Enthused

Natasha is perpetually active, enthused, and vivacious. She represents the childlike energy of youth. Don't dash a child's enthusiasm. It's a cardinal sin. In contrast, adults work hard at being overly calm and restrained. Let your hair down and be full of the fire of youthful enthusiasm. Let the fountain of youth bubble. It is living water.

Natural

To hear the laughter and to see the joy of life in the teenage Natasha is to truly sense woman or man at our uninhibited best. To see and hear the spontaneous joy of the battle-weary Russian soldiers when they discover a clean, refreshing river to bathe in during their retreat is to discover the natural man or woman. They resemble children ecstatically playing in the water at a beach. Reduced to our original, natural selves, we are all alike. Childlike behavior is pure and genuine. Be childlike. Become like children again.

George Bernard Shaw, the English dramatist, put it this way: "Life is a flame that is always burning itself out, but it catches fire again every time a child is born." Larry Barretto described newborns in celestial terms: "Babies are bits of stardust blown from the hand of God. Lucky the woman who knows the pangs of birth, for she has held a star."

God's Way

When God wants a great work done in the
world or a great wrong righted, he goes about
it in a very unusual way. He doesn't stir up his
earthquakes or send forth his thunderbolts.
Instead, he has a helpless baby born, perhaps
in a simple home and of some obscure mother.

*And then God puts the idea into the mother's
heart, and she puts it into the baby's mind.
And then God waits. The greatest forces in the
world are not the earthquakes and the
thunderbolts. The greatest forces in the world
are babies.*

(E.T. Sullivan)

To be real like a child should be a compliment. "And he said: 'I tell you the truth, unless you change and become like little children, you will never enter the kingdom of heaven'" (Matthew 18:2-3 NIV). A child's openness, honesty, and sincerity are unmatched. It takes a formidable woman or man to be so up-front about life. No ulterior motives. No inhibitions. No masks. I'm real, and, yes, human. I make mistakes, but they are honest ones. You can always count on my efforts. Becoming more childlike is not a sign of weakness. Rather, becoming more childlike is to be courageously independent and strong.

Find A Special Place

To have a special place to commune, to pray, to meditate, or simply to relax is essential to meaningful, daily existence. To have a place to think is invaluable. It is a "window to heaven," said Israel Baal Shem Tof. To think about being a traveler, about "Who I really am," and about who these other people really are is fundamental to our figuring out where we belong in the grand scheme of things. Even to think about what is to be learned from a child's uninhibited innocence requires space and time. Find your special place and meditate today.

While vacationing on San Diego Bay, my wife Mamie and I made it a point to take oceanside walks at sunrise. It was as picturesque and meaningful as living on earth can be. However, as good as that was, my favorite vacation spot is undoubtedly Estes Park, Colorado. On John Denver's "Rocky Mountain High," I definitely feel as though I'm walking in the palm of the Creator's hand. It is a great place. It is a slice of heaven. Virgil, the Roman poet, in his *Aeneid*, describes such places this way,

> "He prays to the spirit of the place and to
> Earth, the first of the gods, and to the
> Nymphs and as yet unknown rivers."

Place*: locale, spot, site, space, corner of the world* (Roget's *Super Thesaurus*, 2nd Edition). Where's the best "place" you've ever been? Do you have enough "space"? Do you have a "corner of the world"? What makes these places the best?

Everyone needs a place. A place to get away from it all. A place to slow down. A place to rejuvenate. A place to be lifted up again. A place to find a natural high.

What's your place? Is it your room? Maybe it's the woods. How about a lake or a river or a stream? Is it an empty church? Home? Me? I covet the quiet. I appreciate solitude when I need to rejuvenate. How about you? Charles Cotton said, "Solitude is the soul's best friend." This is the bottom line for having a place, at least temporary solitude. Man is more than a body. Man has also a soul. One sometimes needs the bright light of the sun, the peace and quiet of a secluded place, to come to terms with one's soul.

Here's the good news. One of my favorite places is only a mile from my suburban home. It's on a hill overlooking a high school on one side and a church on the other. It's on a rubberized eight-lane track surrounding a football field. At dusk, it is perfect. Usually, I'm alone. It is quiet. It is peaceful. The sun slowly settles on the horizon like only the art of the Master Painter. Strands and wisps of clouds change shapes and colors as the sun descends. Sometimes the bluebirds are nesting for the day in the adjacent woods. Swallows and finches sit on the fence lines. Flags ripple gently or hang gracefully depending on the wind. It is truly picturesque. Silhouetted against the skyline is the imposing golden steeple of St. Andrew's Church. The Painter listens and talks to me there. Calm and natural, it's a window to paradise. It is a slice of heaven on earth.

I don't need San Diego. I can't go regularly to Estes Park either, but I can escape to the track for a transcendental jog. You too can find "a place" somewhere nearby. A quiet place to maybe exercise and meditate. It is a must for full, enriched living.

In *The Great Gatsby*, George Wilson's friend implores of him after a tragedy, "You gotta find a church, George." Paraphrase: "Readers, you gotta find a *Place!*" A quiet corner of the world helps everyone to keep perspective. Find a place, a refuge, a retreat, a church. There is a Place for each of us. Find it. Commune with your spirit regularly. We all need it. "The Place" will be good for you.

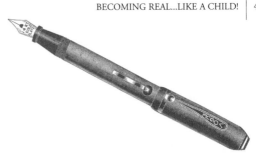

Yesterday, 2005 AD

Post Hip-Hop and R&B-ville, USA

Dear Young People (we've all been there):

John Gay, in *The Beggar's Opera*, writes "Youth's the season made for joy." I suggest a dozen tenets for a joyful youth. I wish I'd shared this list directly with Pam, Kyle, Kim, and Heather, my own children.

The first suggestion is **be respectful**. We all want it. I maintain you get it by giving it. Respect family, siblings, elders, peers, teachers, and employers. You will never go wrong by showing respect to others. Being courteous, taking off your cap, or hat, holding a door, helping out...all are respectful habits which earn you the same respect.

An old athletic axiom says "Respect all; Fear none." It's especially applicable if you're the underdog. How about when we're the favorite? "Respect all; Hurt none." It may be verbal respect. Thumper, in the film *Bambi*, says "If you don't have anything nice to say, don't say anything at all." It may be physical. Lift up. Don't knock down. Remember "There, but for the grace of God, go I." The Golden Rule is golden. "Do unto others as you'd have them do onto you" (Matthew 7:12 NIV). Voltaire, in *Oeuvres,* declares, "We owe respect to the living." It is that simple.

Second, **don't be young and foolish about sex.**

> "Down by the salley gardens my love and I did meet;
> she passed the salley gardens with little snow white feet.
> She bid me take love easy, as the leaves grown on the tree;
> but I, being young and foolish, with her would not agree."

> (W.B. Yeats, "Down by the Salley Gardens")

Love and sex are beautiful and incomprehensible. They are problematic, convoluted, and labyrinthine. Appreciate the complexity of romantic love. Don't be young and foolish. Go slowly. Go respectfully. It is so special. Why not save sex for marriage? The best things in life are worth working for and waiting for. I really believe such self-restraint would reduce the divorce rate too. What if you've already failed the abstinence test? That's understandable in our sex-bombarded society. However, today is the first day of the rest of your life. End the free loving and living today. The best of life is worth the price of sacrificing today's short-lived pleasures for tomorrow's long-term happiness.

Third, **be a friend**. Everyone needs friends. Countless songs, stories, and images remind us. Polonius, in *Hamlet*, tells his son, "Those friends thou hast, and their adoption tried, grapple them onto thy soul with hoops of steel." You get friends by being friendly. Reach out to people, and you'll find they reach back to you.

Fourth, **don't indulge in chemicals**. You don't need hard liquor, beer, nicotine, steroids, cocaine, meth, heroin, or other hard drugs. You don't need any of them. Be real, not unnatural.

"But, but...I'm so down, so blue, so defeated." Well, it is human to have our down days. However, the chemical warfare side-effects and the after-effects aren't worth the temporary high. As one AA member put it, "There is no problem that alcohol won't make worse." Artificial won't last. Be independent, not dependent. Plant your feet while the wind blows hard. You'll be permanently glad you held your ground. The down-day damage is minimal if you dig in and hang tough. You can do it.

Fifth, **give more than you take**. Give more time, love, possessions, and money than you take.

A poor little boy received five pennies. He knew just what he was going to do with his new wealth. He eagerly placed them on the candy-store counter. Quickly placing five candy balls in his pocket, he ran out the door, bound for the Christian Children's Center where he often went to hear the missionary tell stories. The story of that day was of another little boy who gave his lunch to Jesus and because of the gift, many people were fed. He thought of the candy balls in his pocket, took them out, and handed them to the teacher. "I want you to give these to the smaller children here." A good feeling, such as he had never felt before, came over him as he gave the gift. In his later life he said that this incident was one of the turning points for him in developing the philosophy by which he now lived.

Give gladly, young people. Don't be just a taker from this world. Give back. It's a pivotal premise. It's a perfect invisible principle.

Sixth, **keep hours that are beneficial to body, mind, and spirit.** Someone once told me anything that can't be done by midnight can wait until the next day. The body isn't strengthened, the mind isn't sharpened, and the spirit isn't heightened by the wee morning hours.

Seventh, **drive carefully.** Oh, to get that driver's license. Independence, freedom, mobility, maturity. Wheels are awesome, so be awe-inspired. Drive well. Drive defensively. Drive patiently. For good reason people describe high speeds as "breakneck" speeds. And road rage is outrageous. Get real. Who wins from reckless driving? No one! Be sensible.

Eighth, **learn as much as possible.** In *The Merchant of Venice*, Shakespeare describes a young person: "I never knew so young a body with so old a head." The mind is unbelievably capable if given the chance. Knowledge is power. Knowledge, plus experience, is real learning. Be book and street smart. You'll never regret intellectual growth.

Ninth, **experience as many activities as you can.** Experience broadens one's life and perspective. Try different types of music, different sports, different types of entertainment, different foods, different books. There is spice in variety. So many places to visit. So many interesting people, each with an original story. Experience life as fully as you can. Drink deeply of life. Its nectar is sweet and fulfilling beyond your imagination. Savor as many experiences as you can.

Tenth, **don't work too much.** You'll be working more than 40 hours per week soon enough. Young people holding jobs is one of the scourges of modern day society, I believe. It diminishes your likelihood of academic excellence; it physically wears you down; it depletes your opportunities to experience a variety of activities; it socially handicaps you. Where's John Gay's "youthful season made for joy"?

Are young people better off internally for holding a job? I said *internally*! No! Don't tell me it's necessary in many cases. Money yanks our heads around to cockeyed positions. We prostitute our existences chasing the almighty dollar. Do "taste" the job world. But make it a taste, not a meal. A few hours of work experience can be educational too. Good, let's experience it, but let's not ruin the joy of youth by becoming 20-to-50-hour-a-week workaholics. "Money is a good servant, but a bad master," said Henry Bohn. May it only serve your joyous youth.

Eleventh, **act like a role model for the innocent ones who follow in your footsteps.** "There are little eyes upon you." Like it or not, you are a role model for siblings, neighbors, and strangers. They watch you drive, shop, play, perform, and live. Model well, young men and women. The innocent ones need positive role models.

Twelfth, **join a church.** A church teaches us *JOY*: *J*esus first, *O*thers second, and *Y*ourself last.

John Wooden of the University of California at Los Angeles, the holder of more Division I college basketball titles than any other coach, once told me to "drink deeply from good books. If you can only have one, the Bible will suffice." Similarly, young America, if you can only follow one of these tenets, make it number twelve. Hang your hat, bet the moon, go for broke with the Church. Follow Mother Teresa. You will have joy in your heart.

God is like Bayer Aspirin... He works wonders.
    God is like Pepsi... He's got a lot to give.
    God is like Ford... He's got a better idea.
    God is like Dial soap... He gives
        around-the-clock protection.
    God is like Coke... He's the "real thing."
    God is like Sun Country... He makes the going great.
    God is like Scope... He keeps you fresh all day
    God is like Hallmark... He cared enough
        to send the very best.
    (Author Unknown)

Hey, I've been there too. Yes, I've walked in your shoes. It is a great time, but it's also surely a challenging time. Work hard on knowing who you are and what you truly believe in. Then, be strong. I wish I were there with you.

Best Wishes,

A Former Youth

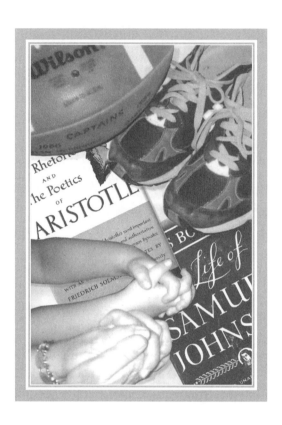

"*People go into this world with well-developed bodies, fairly developed minds, and undeveloped hearts.*"

- E. M. Forster

CHAPTER FOUR

Becoming Three-Dimensional

The Russian novelist Fyodor Dostoyevsky answers our "Who are we? Who am I?" questions in his classic work, *The Brothers Karamazov*. He suggests that man is three dimensional: physical, intellectual, and spiritual. He illustrates these dimensions through his main characters: Dmitri, the primarily physical, worldly brother; Ivan, the primarily intellectual, scholarly brother; and Alyosha, the primarily spiritual, monastic brother. In the course of the novel, each wrestles with the three dimensions, just as you and I do. Our lives combine the three dimensions, and we need a balance among them.

In *Hamlet,* Shakespeare makes a similar point:

> What a piece of work is a man, how noble in reason,
> how infinite in faculties, in form and moving, how express
> and admirable in action, how like an angel in apprehension,
> how like a god: the beauty of the world; the paragon of animals.

(Act II, Sc. 2, L289)

If you and I accept the principles of three-dimensional living, then we have a road map to guide our travels. We have identified "Who We Are" and where we are. Having done so, we should readily find purpose for where we are going and should have ample reasons for what we are doing. To get up in the morning, come rain or come shine, with purpose and meaning is good. It is Becoming. Let's examine those three-dimensional possibilities.

THE PHYSICAL DIMENSION

Physical: of or pertaining to the body, as distinguished from the mind or spirit; bodily; corporeal; pertaining to material things; pertaining to matter and energy.

"Let's get physical." "Have you had a physical lately?" "What a physique!" "Men, we need to be more physical in the second half." A TV special recently was illustrating the ways the sexes (man or animal) are attracted to each other and/or court each other. Physical playfulness is indigenous to all species. Nudging, poking, tickling, jabbing...touching...as a prelude to more intimate physical endearments. Human sexuality is certainly physical. It embodies the ultimate highs and lows of man's nature.

How are we feeling at this moment? Physically robust and energetic? Worn-out or run-down? Clear breathing today, or sinus-plagued, or snotty-nosed? How about those wisdom teeth? Is your heartbeat patiently pulsating healthfully? Does your heart murmur arythmatically, beating rapidly for little reason? Feeling nauseous, starved, bloated? How about your eyes, ears, skin, stomach, legs, feet?

What a piece of work we are! Circulatory, nervous, respiratory, digestive, and reproductive systems. Voluntary and involuntary muscle responses. Foods and liquids turn into useful by-products and waste materials. An eye records an image and passes it to the brain, which triggers a nervous or muscular response. A scrape or cut leads to coagulation, a scab, healing, and new skin. And reproductive capabilities?! An egg and sperm unite to create a new organism, a new life, a new human being. Don't we take the physical for granted?

One of the *H's* in a 4-H member's pledge is health. Health, what a gift. Flu, ingrown toe nail, sprained ankle, swollen knee, eye problems, headache: these are the minor health concerns. Hair, teeth, bones, muscles, organs. Covet your health. Cherish your physicality.

Are you cold? Are you hot? Do you like the smell of burning wood? How about a gentle mountain breeze across a lake? Eternity perfume or Gucci after-shave? The sliminess of a fish in your hand; the warmth of a child's hand clutched in yours. The taste of a charcoaled steak, the taste of a jalapeno bagel with garlic spread. The feeling after a vigorous physical workout: blood circulating, salty sweat in eyes and mouth, a pleasantly fatigued sensation. These sensations are physical.

Dmitri was the physical man. "Eat, drink, and be merry." But the physical alone wasn't enough. He had intellectual and spiritual questions too. Dmitri, the wild one, the "crazy guy," ultimately finds his peace when he accepts the compatibility of all three dimensions of our lives.

THE INTELLECTUAL, MENTAL DIMENSION

Intellectual: the ability to learn and reason as distinguished from the ability to feel or will; capacity for knowledge and understanding; the ability to think abstractly or profoundly.

I think I can. I think I can. I think I can. With these words, the tiny engine in *The Little Engine That Could* reached the crest of the hill. With a puff and a snort, it started down the incline with the happy refrain, "I thought I could. I thought I could. I thought I could." It picked up speed with every affirmation.

Norman Vincent Peale sold millions of copies of his book called *The Power of Positive Thinking*. Transactional analysts ask us to accept ourselves. One book title tells us *I'm OK, You're OK*. Accept yourself. Think you can. Be positive. As Henry Ford put it, "Whether you think you can, or whether you think you can't, you're right."

The mind is a gift. If you dream it, you can achieve it. Architecture, space exploration, medicine, artistic masterpieces. Do you know most people tap their minds for only 12–15% of their potential? Be thankful for minds well-used.

As a high school coach of forty-seven years, I guarantee you that the mind is at least as important as the body. In fact, I think it is more important. Consider the father who tilts upright an overturned tractor pinning his son under it after a farming accident! The man who lifts a car's axle when a friend is immobilized under it in a tire-changing mishap. Rocky Balboa versus the Russian boxer. The U.S. Olympic hockey miracle of 1980. Wilbur and Orville Wright initiating the saga of men and machines flying through the heavens...to the moon, to Mars, and to space stations. Oh, the power of our minds.

What happens when powerful minds become proud, corrupt, and abusive? A Tower of Babel. A Master Race of human beings. Brainwashed minds vulnerable to suggestions, as in the Jonestown mass suicides. Assault, rape, murder, perversion, political greed, ethnic cleansing, government corruption, prostitution, vice lords, terrorism. These are examples of proud, arrogant, thoughtless, remorseless, bitter thinking. The mind used? No, the mind abused for devious causes and purposes. Oh, the power of the corrupt minds.

As an educator, I had my teaching highs when students used all of their intellectual capacities. Just use it all. Conversely, the teaching lows were the lazy underachievers. I invariably marveled at the majority of the students from abroad especially from Asia, who were acclimating themselves to the United States. Their diligence, attention to detail, exactitude, and work habits were exemplary. In contrast, a lot of homegrown students were cruising and unappreciative of their educational opportunities. Use it or lose it: muscle or minds. If the mind is nourished, it will flourish. If it's not fed or challenged, it will shrivel or die.

By now, your mind is working. You are assuredly thinking. You are processing. You are selectively thinking, what's for me? You are intellectualizing these thoughts. You're comparing your perspective to my perspective. Now, I maintain thinkers may have more trouble in life than non-thinkers. They have a lot of material in their "think tanks," and they have to sort it out, organize it, and process it. In Tennessee Williams' play *Cat on a Hot Tin Roof*, Big Daddy says, "A man doesn't have a pig's advantage. Ignorance of mortality is a comfort." A pig doesn't worry about dying. A human being might. We think about which ice cream flavor to order, but we also ponder our physical, intellectual, and spiritual dimensions.

Ivan in *The Brothers Karamazov* epitomizes this "paralysis of analysis." He analyzes everything. He's too serious. He broods as he over-intellectualizes his job, his father, his brother Smerdyakov, his own personal life, Dmitri's physicality, and Alyosha's spirituality. Think, but don't overthink. Think, study, analyze, and live.

THE SPIRITUAL DIMENSION

Spiritual: the vital principle or animating force within human beings; of, concerned with, or affecting the soul; of, from, pertaining to God; vitality, force, soul, life, God.

Spirit, vitality, strength, force, life, God! The intangible strength of units. The cheerleaders' spirit. The spirit of the immigrants crossing an ocean. The pioneering spirit. The Spirit of 1776. Team spirit. Spiritual music. Vital, forceful, soul-moving, God-fearing spirit.

E.M. Forster said, "People go forth into the world with well-developed bodies, fairly developed minds, and undeveloped hearts."

Dostoyevsky, like many of us, wrestled with his physical nature, tried to intellectualize his experiences, and explored his spirituality. *The Brothers Karamazov* is a lifetime reflection on these battles.

*I thirst for life... but I am base... I am torn between
the ideal of the Madonna and the ideal of Sodom... the
whole world stands on absurdities... suffering is life...
what becomes of harmony? I'm a scoundrel, but not a thief
... it's always worthwhile speaking to a clever man...
if man is defined by freedom, then freedom constitutes man's
greatest burden... heaven lies hidden within all of us...
without suffering, what would be the pleasure of life...
no law of nature that man should love mankind... I think
everyone should love life above everything in the world...
there is no God, then all is lawful... there's no law of nature
that man should love mankind... what is hell? I maintain
it's the incapacity to love.*

(Fyodor Dostoyevsky, cuttings from *The Brothers Karamazov*)

The toughest part of the Karamazov brothers' story is the intangible quality of the spiritual side of life. We mortals like the tangible. We sometimes have trouble with the intangible: what we can't touch, feel, smell, taste, and see. The ancient Greeks acknowledged that there is "Something out there bigger and greater than humans." The Greeks believed that some larger reason, order, and intelligibility animates the cosmos. Mount Olympus, Zeus, and the hierarchy of the gods were attempts at making tangible the intangible world of the spirit.

Is there or isn't there a spiritual side to me too? Is there or isn't there a God? My personal experience with the ups and downs of life which all of us experience is that when I ignore the spiritual, I'm the least satisfied. At those times, I'm at my loneliest, my love lessens, my purpose wanders, and I'm most apt to be alienated. The wisdom of Ecclesiastes suggests that at least some features of life and existence are predictable and orderly.

> A time to be born and a time to die,
> A time to plant and a time to uproot,
> A time to kill and a time to heal,
> A time to tear down and a time to build,
> A time to weep and a time to laugh,
> A time to mourn and a time to dance,
> A time to scatter stones and a time to gather them,
> A time to embrace and a time to refrain.
> A time to search and a time to give up,
> A time to keep and a time to give away,
> A time to tear and a time to mend,
> A time to be silent and a time to speak,
> A time to love and a time to hate,
> A time for war and a time for peace.
>
> (*Ecclesiastes* 3:2-8 NIV)

As we continue our travels in the new millennium, can we really attribute it all to the Big Bang theory? From the wonder of human physiology, from seed to harvest, from sunrise to sunset, from winter to summer, from tears of sadness to tears of joy, from cells to atoms... it's too orderly, too rational, too intelligible to be only an explosion.

Somewhere, somehow we must make a leap of faith. Biblical literature quotes Jesus Christ in his teachings as saying the following about the spirit: "Flesh gives birth to flesh but the Spirit gives birth to spirit. The wind blows wherever it pleases. You hear its sound, but you cannot tell where it comes from or where it's going. So it is with everyone born of the Spirit" (John 3:6, 8 NIV). "The spirit gives life; the flesh counts for nothing" (John 6:63 NIV).

Ivan of *The Brothers Karamazov* needs a leap of faith to understand what Alyosha accepts and what Dmitri eventually comes to realize. There is a segue needed. There's a synapse to be jumped. Can I make the spiritual leap of faith? Without Big Daddy's pig's advantage, serious thinkers such as Ivan are at a crossroads. Who am I? Who are we? Is it worth going down an uncharted road?

In *Candida* George Bernard Shaw writes, "It is easy...terribly easy... to shake a man's faith in himself. To take advantage of that, to break a man's spirit is devil's work." Have you seen a street person? Have you seen a horse who has been "broken" or the bull tormented into apathy by the toreador? Have you pictured Pavlov's dog with the bell ringing but no meat provided? Have you seen people try to drown themselves in alcohol and drugs because of broken spirits? When negative, the human spirit can become an abominable abyss. In contrast, a positive spirit is as awe-inspiring as a Rocky Mountain snowcap. It is vibrant, lively, soul-felt, and godly.

The hymn begins, "Spirit of God, descend on me today." Rev. Roger Eigenfeld in a daily devotional that he wrote for his parishioners shared an anecdote of the spirit descending:

A woman came home one day to find herself face to face with a burglar. She dropped her groceries and attempted to run out the door only to be stopped by the man, slamming and locking the door trapping her inside her own house. Not knowing what the man was capable of doing, she began to fear for her life. She felt her worst fears were about to be realized. Then it happened. Suddenly she realized there were not two people in that house, but three. The third was her Lord Jesus. It's something she had never felt before; yet it was real. The helper she needed was there. At first her words were soft and silent: "Lord Jesus, help me! Lord Jesus, help me!" But then her sentence became more audible as she looked the man straight in the eye, and with a calmness that had to come from the very hand of God himself, she said, "Lord Jesus, I know you are here, come and help me."

The man looked over his shoulder. His eyes raced to take in every corner of the room. Suddenly he raced for the door. Unlocking it, he mouthed the words, "I'm sorry, lady. I'm sorry." And then he was gone.

Spiritual strength is immeasurable. Its power is unsurpassed.

Pearl Buck in her short story, "The Old Demon," has characterized an indomitable spirit too in an elderly lady named Mrs. Wang. The setting is the Yellow River Valley of China in 1937. The Japanese are invading. The Old Demon is the river.

"That river...it was full of good and evil. It would water the fields when it was curbed and checked. But if an inch was allowed it, it cracked through like a roaring lion." Her husband had died in it years before when the dike had broken. Mrs. Wang's house is gone from the bombing. Everyone is evacuating except for her. "At her age, she need be afraid of nothing." She finds a wounded Japanese pilot and begins to take care of him. "It would be nice if I could find something for us to eat." When she returns from the ruins of a baker's shop with four rolls, he has died. "She climbed the dike slowly, getting very hot. She was shocked to see the river was near the top of the dike, why it had risen in the last hour! 'You Old Demon,' she said. Then just as she was about to climb down, she saw something on the eastern horizon. At first, it was only an immense cloud of dust. As she stared at it, very quickly it became a lot of black dots and shiny spots. It was a lot of men...an army, the Japanese. Buzzing silver planes were over them. "I don't know who you're looking for, unless it's me, and Little Pig and his wife and seven kids. You've already killed my brother Pao. Maybe you've killed them too!"

She was about halfway down when she thought of the water gate. This old river...it had been a curse to them since time began. Why should it not make up a little now for all the wickedness it had done? She wavered a moment. It was a pity, of course, that the dead Japanese would be swept away into the flood. He was a nice looking boy and she had tried to save him. She went over to him and tugged at him until he lay near the top of the bank. Then she went down again.

She knew how to open the gate. Any child knew how to open the sluice for crops. The question was could she open it quickly enough to get out of the way? I'm only one old woman. She turned resolutely to the gate. Some people fought with airplanes and some with guns, but you could fight with a river too. She wrenched out one of the huge wooden pins. A rill of water burst into a strong jet. When she wrenched one more pin, the rest would give way of themselves. She pulled at it and felt it begin to slip from the hole.

I might be able to get myself out of purgatory with this, she thought, and maybe they'll let me have that old man of mine too. What's a foot of his to all this? Then we'll...The pin slipped away suddenly and the gate burst flat against her and knocked her breath away. She had, only time to gasp to the river, 'Come on, you Old Demon.'

Then she felt it seize her and left her up to the sky. It was beneath her, around her. It rolled her joyfully hither and thither; then, holding her close and enfolded, it went rushing against the enemy."

The Negro spiritual echoes this closing, "Old Man River, he just keeps rolling." Pearl Buck's ironic line, "Joyfully, it rolled her hither and thither" is a peaceful spiritual epitaph to Mrs. Wang who became one with the spirit of the river.

We are three-dimensional beings, yet free to make choices. Physically, do you love or lust? Intellectually, are you cerebral or carnal? Spirituality, are you theistic or atheistic? Your choices may mean war or peace, harmony or cacophony. Becoming intellectually, spiritually, and physically vigorous is to be truly healthy. Experiencing that is a giant step towards reaching our true potential. Three-dimensional power is real muscle.

Four Things a Person Must Learn To Do

Four things a person must learn to do to live a life that's true:

1. To think without confusion clearly
2. To love your fellowman sincerely
3. To act from honest motives purely
4. To trust in God and heaven securely

In forty-seven years as a high school teacher and coach, I have stood on the sidelines and awaited the start of approximately 1,200 varsity contests. Before most I silently repeated the above poem as the National Anthem played. It has helped my focus. In hindsight, if I had known this verse all my life, I would have repeated it before dates, before choosing a college, before choosing a career, before marriage, before funerals, before all my choices of leisure time activities. Why? Same four reasons. Try it. It's timeless. Life's a challenge. Come prepared. It's an unbeatable game plan.

To Think Without Confusion Clearly

Set aside the emotions of the moment. Focus solely and objectively on the task at hand. Lock out the past, the distractions and the worries. *Carpe diem.*

To Love Your Fellowman Sincerely

I maintain all rivals should periodically "break bread" together. This could be business, ideological, political, sporting, or theological rivals. No one but your rivals can empathize as well with you as the competition. "Breaking bread together" tears down walls of non-communication and explodes misconceptions about the "enemy." As we pass the food and share together, we see each other as we really are:

just plain people pursuing common dreams. Appreciate your fellow-man because we are all travelers on the road of life.

To Act From Honest Motives Purely

If my motives are pure and honest, my actions must be beyond reproach. No corners cut. No rules broken to gain advantage. Fairness to all. Do it right the first time. That's a pure, honest principle. No matter the issue—dating, marriage, parenting, buying, selling—just do it right the first time.

To Trust In God and Heaven Securely

I need to trust in the Master Coach, the Creator of the Universe. That's enough.

Think clearly, love sincerely, act purely, and trust securely in all your decisions and endeavors. Trust that your words, deeds, examples, and influences will be positive. If we follow these four steps, then, we will have acted deliberately, honorably, and with principle. And that's the best we can do.

"*We can believe what we choose.*
We are answerable for what we choose to believe."

- Cardinal Newman

CHAPTER FIVE

Becoming a Believer

*H*aving a belief system to guide our daily lives is a vital first step to becoming all that we are capable of being. An equally important second step is to have an accessible support group, in person or by inspiration, to lean on in times of crisis. This chapter exemplifies both. The assertions are based on my belief that there is an Eternal Father who can "still the waters." One of the hymns sung at President John F. Kennedy's funeral echoes that conviction:

> Eternal Father, strong to save,
> Whose arm has bound the restless wave,
> Who bade the mighty ocean deep
> It's own appointed limits keep
> Oh, hear us when we cry to thee
> For those in peril on the sea
>
> (*Lutheran Book of Worship* #467)

Jane Froman and her team of writers, particularly Ervin Drake, created the song, "I Believe," for a serviceman in Korea in 1952. Drake said it was intended to "give the average person hope." Every human being needs a belief system to have hope.

"I believe for every drop of rain that falls, a flower grows.
I believe that somewhere in the darkest night, a candle glows.
I believe for everyone who goes astray,
someone will come to show the way.
I believe above the storm the smallest prayer will still be heard.
I believe that someone in the great somewhere hears every word.
Every time I hear a newborn baby cry, or touch a leaf,
or see the sky...then I know why I believe!"

What do you believe? Whom do you believe? In what and in whom do you put your hope? *BELIEVE*: "to have faith or confidence in the truth, value, or existence of something; to accept as true (*American Heritage Dictionary*)." King Solomon was universally respected for his wisdom. He wrote in the book of Proverbs:

"Get wisdom, get understanding. Do not forsake wisdom and she will protect you; love her and she will watch over you. Get understanding, esteem her and she will exalt you; embrace her and she will honor you. I guide you in the ways of wisdom and lead you along straight paths. When you walk, your steps will not be hampered; when you run, you will not stumble."

(Proverbs 4: 5-8, 11-12, NIV)

Belief. Wisdom. Understanding. Altogether, I'd call it becoming.

We need something to believe in for life to have meaning. Without a philosophy, I'm rudderless. Without a creed or religion to follow, I become amoral. Without morality, I am irresponsible. Without responsibility, I'm careless. I need understanding, insight, and wisdom.

Without them, I'm clueless. Cardinal Newman, in volume 12 of his *Letters and Diaries of John Henry Newman*, succinctly puts it this way, "We can believe what we choose. We are answerable for what we choose to believe."

Life without meaning may foreshadow suicide. A high school friend despairs of life after a breakup with a girl friend. A gifted high school English student decides "*It...isn't worth living.*" A youth evangelist with a disability commits suicide. While pheasant hunting as a 9-year-old in southern Minnesota, my boyhood buddy and I find a man who has hanged himself. Ernest Hemingway and so on. The unknown and the well-known. Despair plays no favorites. Our beliefs, our philosophies, our creeds must be strong enough to withstand the tornadoes and monsoons of life. One of my deep beliefs: If *what* we believe is not supported by *whom* we believe, we can be vulnerable.

Horace, the classical poet of 65 BC, emphatically cited the value of having a belief system in one of his odes, "Believe me, you who come after me!" The context of this could have been in reference to how to write, but the admonition is *Believe*, "hang your hat," accept as true, "keep the faith."

I believe a good, happy life must be rooted in love. Everyone needs someone to love. Everyone needs someone to be loved by. Everyone needs something to love to do. First Corinthians 13, the "perfect love" chapter of the New Testament, is the backbone of this simple philosophy. I really believe it's a foolproof formula. Let's examine the three premises.

Someone To Love

We all need someone to love, someone to give to. Giving is good. Giving because we love is beautiful. Most of us get our first opportunities to love someone through our parents. Obviously, it isn't always there, but the opportunity for a child to bring a dandelion bouquet into the house for Mom or to hand Dad the hammer as he builds a bench in the garage are small acts of love. Then maybe this type of love is passed on to an elementary school teacher: a chance to help him or her with cleaning erasers, feeding goldfish, bringing in the flag, and so on. Give of time, words, and acts today too.

Love your friends. If I could live in a perfect neighborhood, with all due respects to my present neighbors, I'd like to have a grade-school-through-high-school friend, a college roommate, and a professional friend each live within several houses of mine. Alas, one lives in California, one in Colorado, and one on the other side of the Twin Cities. Why would I want them nearby? Because I have experienced a lot of life with all three, have shared the highs and lows of life with all three, and have loved life with all three. As Polonius tells his son Laertes in Shakespeare's play, *Hamlet*, "Those friends thou hast, and their adoption tried, grapple them onto thy soul with hoops of steel."

Love the opposite sex. What could be better than two people going out of their ways to be good to each other, to care for each other, to be concerned for each other, to physically be loving to each other? And, if that latter act is enhanced through marriage with the chance to become proud parents, proud of the two becoming three or more, then all the better.

Hal David said it well in Burt Bacharach's song, "What the world needs now is love, sweet love." A baby needs someone to love. An orphan needs someone to love. The elderly need someone to love. The derelict needs someone to love. We all need someone to love. Without someone to believe in, to have faith in, to care about, we despair. We lack purpose. We are nothing. How sad is the oft-repeated story of elderly couples wherein one dies and within six months the other one dies too: no one, and seemingly nothing, to live for. Love: the unequivocal desire to share another's ups and downs of life.

If one can't find someone mortal to love, an Immortal will more than satisfy. A Supreme Being can be loved, counted on, shared with, and served. Humans who undergird all they believe and do with faith in Someone bigger than man are never desperate when fellow mortals disappoint them. John Coltrane called this "a love supreme." The beautiful, loving act of giving to others, mortal or immortal, is fundamental to a happy, good life.

John Greenleaf Whittier, in his poem, "Maud Miller" said, "For of all sad words of tongue or pen, the saddest are these, 'It might have been'." Did you ever tell someone of your love, and that person paused, stammered, and avoided responding? We are often reluctant to express our love, feeling we might be put down, or laughed at. However, never be too proud to say, "I love you." As Meyer Wolfsheim said in F. Scott Fitzgerald's *The Great Gatsby,* "Let us learn to show our friendship for a man when he is alive and not after he is dead." I remember the long distance telephone call telling me that my father had had a heart attack and had died instantly. "No, wait...tell me he's dying. I want to speed down the highway and tell him I loved him even more than he thought." Don't be hesitant to say "I love you" if you mean it. Don't be fragile if it isn't returned. You cared enough to share it.

Someone To Be Loved By

From where might we receive unconditional love? Yes, from parents and family. Yes, from friends of both sexes. Yes, from support groups like teams, clubs, study groups, and counseling groups. We aren't lemmings, but as Reuben Welch's great little poetic book, *We Really Do Need Each Other,* says, we do need the assemblies of "Family," "Friends," and "Groups." Listen to the lyrics of the song:

> Everybody needs a bit of friendship,
> Friendship that is tried and true,
> Everybody, everywhere must have it,
> Every day the whole year through.

> (*4-H Friendship Song*)

We do need each other. We do need to know someone cares. Words, touches, gifts, looks, smiles, tears, applause: they all tell me I am loved. Do you have any idea how much that dog thrives on your pausing in your busy paths to pat it, even once or twice, on the head? If you recognize that, then I know you do it regularly! We thrive on love too. We die emotionally without love. Somebody to be loved by. Yes!

Something To Love To Do

When I was five, it was really fun to dig this "big" hole in the yard with my toy shovel. When I was fifteen, it was a lot of fun to shoot hundreds of jump shots because I was getting better. When I was twenty-five, it was great coaching high schoolers to shoot jump shots as they got better. When I was thirty-five, it was fun teaching our own children to sing, dance, catch, and throw. When I was forty-five, it was great to make Greek plays, Tolstoy, Dostoyevsky, Shakespeare, Faulkner, O'Neill, Williams, Malamud, and Hemingway come alive for college-bound students. At fifty-five, it was awesome for my wife and me to appreciate thirty-three years of a good marriage and four fine, grown children. Today? Another generation to love: six grandchildren. The fun and the love are deeper, better, and more appreciated than ever.

How can I love what I'm doing? Consider trying the five simple tenets of "A Good Life of Loving What I Do." First, do meaningful work. It could be manual labor or mental labor. Sweat from either is worthwhile if they are labors of love. Maybe you can show your love by leading, or, at least, supporting your coworkers. That's love too.

Second, make loving and giving a daily activity. You give to your job, your products, your coworkers, your employers, your affiliates, your contacts. Giving is loving. When I give, I forget myself and put others first. Gayle Sayers, the great Chicago Bears tailback and roommate of cancer-stricken Brian Piccolo, commemorated his teammate in the book, *I Am Third*: God first, others second, myself last. It works. Give lovingly to whatever you do. Expect nothing in return.

Third, exercise daily. Love yourself enough to workout because it tones both body and mind. Exertion stimulates, invigorates, enhances your creativity, and gives you time for meditation. I heard a cardiologist and heart transplant surgeon give a thrilling and frightening speech entitled "Hearts Made of Stone." He told us if we do not physically sweat every forty-eight hours, then a doctor's chances of saving our clogged plumbing—our hearts made of stone—were poor. We guiltily wanted to sneak out of the auditorium to begin jogging. Exercise is a gift to your job, your loved ones, and yourself. Take a "brisk walk" at lunch time. Perform isometrics at your desk. "Just do it," as the Nike ads tell us. You'll be better off in every way for this time well-spent.

Fourth, make time to grow. Paint. Read. Visit theaters and museums. Enjoy concerts. Travel. Go and grow in diverse ways. Growth breeds confidence.

Finally, meditate daily. I suppose you could practice yoga or stare out across a lake from a cabin. I suggest instead a quiet time of prayer and reading. Pray to your God. Yes, there's a given here: there is a God. I'm much lonelier, more helpless, more alienated, less loving, less self-sufficient, and less creative, when my connection to God is weak. In contrast, whenever I find time to meditate, read the scriptures for inspiration, and pray, then I become much more productive, tolerant, understanding, and forgiving. On those days I give more, take less, gain more, and multiply happiness around me.

Tom Osborne, the extremely successful University of Nebraska football coach, retired and entered politics after 25 years as a head coach. He won 255 games, lost 49, and tied 3 in his career—a winning percentage of 83.5%. We should all "win" so well! In the February 1998 issue of *Sharing the Victory*, he spoke of trying to maintain 20-30 minutes of prayer or meditation twice a day, a short time of scripture study before breakfast, a weekly Bible study, and regular worship at his church. Coach Osborne said,

> "In the book of Isaiah, it says that 'those who wait upon the Lord will renew their strength. They will mount up with wings like eagles. They will run and not grow weary, they will walk and not faint.' I know that God provides the necessary strength to those who desire to serve Him. Tom Landry, the legendary Dallas Cowboy football coach, once said, 'to live a disciplined life, and to accept the result of that disciplined life as the will of God is the mark of a man.' "

As a career teacher and coach, these role models inspire me. If these practices are good enough for men like these, they should be good enough for me. I trust these people. I believe in their values. How about you? You can find role models in your vocation and avocation too!

Honor the above-mentioned five tenets, and I'll wager your life will never be the same, even if it's good now! On the other hand, with the nay-sayers of the world surrounding us with cynical, self-centered, desperate, and apathetic comments, we are certainly at times skeptical, doubtful, and disillusioned. Your beliefs will be challenged and challenging. That's all the more reason for faith. Faith evolves from love; love denotes sharing; sharing may be a struggle; struggle requires faith. Hannah Whitall Smith once wrote, "Sight is not faith, and hearing is not faith, neither is feeling faith; but believing when we neither see, hear, nor feel is faith…Therefore, we must believe before we feel, and often against our feelings if we would honor God by our faith."

Here are four magic words to build your day around: "**I believe in you!**" If faith could tell you that God believes in you, it would be the ultimate affirmation. If you know you have a support group who also believe in your worth, those same words are golden. Ultimately, believe in yourself too. "I believe in myself." Say it out loud. You have a right to affirm that belief. The past is history. Carry neither garbage nor garlands. This future starts this moment. You can because you think you can. We can because we believe in each other. Believe. When you sincerely say "I believe in you" to someone else, then they may throw their shoulders back and look to the sun, too.

Having a belief system and having friends who also believe are indispensable steps to a happy, fulfilling life. Becoming a believer takes strength of character because it does involve a leap of faith, and our world wants to dwell on tangibles, not intangibles. However, the will to trust and believe gives backbone and substance to one's life. The power of becoming a believer is not man-made power. It is Supreme Power.

PRAY Is An Acronym

Prayer is clearly superior to worry, a psychiatrist says. In the *American Journal of Psychiatry*, Dr. Alan Challman, clinical professor emeritus at the University of Minnesota medical school, says that worry is a compulsive pagan prayer. Worry "is unconsciously instigated mental activity that seeks to control fate through suffering," he says. "Prayer," he continues, "is an alternative to worry since it also appeals to supernatural powers for helpful intercession. Prayer is clearly superior since it involves much less suffering and can be started and stopped at will." Or, as Bobby McFerrin sings "Don't worry. Be happy." As Lord Alfred Tennyson expressed it in *Idylls of the King*, "More things are wrought by prayer than this world dreams of."

I think prayer requires two basic premises: (1) recognition of and reliance on Something or Someone bigger than man and (2) love of that Force or God, of fellowman, and of self. Prayer is appropriate at any time, in any way, and in any place. When I was young, someone told me that the best posture for prayer was "the attitude of gratitude," on one's knees with folded hands. Most of us need to get on our knees more often than we do, whether it is for praise or for requests. That particular, totally dependent posture is good for us because it is humbling. We're totally reliant there. I've used it in my most desperate moments. I need to use it at other times too.

However, wherever and whenever you choose to pray, be humble and sincere. Speak from your heart. Pray about anything. Listen to James, Jesus' brother, "You do not have, because you do not ask" (James 4:2 NIV). John, the disciple "whom Jesus loved," puts it this way, "Ask and you will receive, and your joy will be complete" (John 16:24 NIV). That sounds awesome, doesn't it? Nevertheless, one restriction: leave purely selfish petitions at the door. James continues, "When you ask, you do not receive because you ask with wrong mo-tives, that you may spend what you get on your pleasures" (James 4:3 NIV). In the book of Matthew, Jesus himself says, "If you believe, you will receive whatever you ask for in prayer" (Matthew 21:22 NIV). Pray diligently "Thy will be done" and truly expect answers in God's due time.

We have been blessed. Hopefully, we're blessed to be a blessing to the world and all its needs. Humbly, seek the continued grace of such gifts through prayer requests. Reliance on a Supreme Being should result in communion with God. Abraham Heschel called prayer "A ladder on which thoughts mount to God." Samuel Coleridge described prayer simply and clearly in *The Rime of the Ancient Mariner:*

> He prayeth well, who loveth well
> Both man and bird and beast,
> He prayeth best, who loveth best,
> All things both great and small.

I think of prayer as a four-step endeavor, made easy to remember by a simple acronym.

P *Praise* first, give thanks for specific blessings and joys of life.
R *Repent,* confess failings and shortcomings.
A pray for *All others.*
Y pray for *Yourself* last.

Praise

Pray thankfully when awaking in the morning, when shaving, when driving, while working, at bedtime. There are a quadrillion little things to be thankful for: rays of sun through the venetian blinds, berries on cereal, a kiss from a loved one, a clear raindrop on a verdant leaf. How many, how long? G. E. Lessing, in his play *Mina von Barnhelm,* answers it precisely, "One single, grateful thought raised to heaven is the most perfect prayer." That may be enough.

Repent

We do things wrong…acts of commission. Ask forgiveness. We fail to do things…acts of omission. Ask forgiveness. What have we done poorly? What haven't we done?

All Others

It is joyful to see other people's lives benefit from our prayers. Surely, you're going to include family and extended family in praying for others, but make it a point to include the needs of lesser known people, and even relatively unknown people among your requests. Needs you've spotted coincidentally are needs too: the daily, perhaps lonely, brisk walker; the street person as you drive or walk through the city; the young mother on the residential doorstep with obviously four children under six years of age surrounding her. There are others with needs everywhere. Pray for them.

Yourself

Have you ever noticed how caring for others first sometimes lessens the importance of our own needs? Praising, confessing, and praying for others initially should help us to focus our petitions. It should help us keep our personal requests to meat-and-potatoes issues. However, don't be afraid to ask for anything at any time. Be specific and believe that it will be heard. Underscore your prayer with, "and Your will be done." Listen again to the Apostle John,

> This is the confidence we have in approaching God:
> that if we ask anything according to His Will, he hears us.
> And if we know that he hears us…whatever we ask…
> we know that we have what we asked of Him.
>
> (I John 5:14-15 NIV)

Pray confidently. Pray conversationally. Pray frequently. PRAY. Pray as if everything depends on God, then work as if everything depends on you.

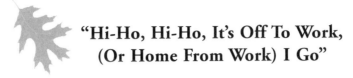

"Hi-Ho, Hi-Ho, It's Off To Work, (Or Home From Work) I Go"

The Seven Dwarfs had the right attitude as they sang and whistled their way off to work and home from work each day. Music is a source for inspiration, meditation, and relaxation. It could be as you prepare for work or play, for Quiet Time, or for recreation. It definitely can help us have a healthy mind set for whatever we are about to do.

Billy Rose and Edward Ilescu wrote the lyrics for a great melody entitled "Without a Song." It testifies to music's universality. "Without a song, the day would never end. Without a song, the road would never bend. When things go wrong, a man ain't got a friend without a song."

When I was about ten years old, a Walt Disney movie entitled "With a Song in My Heart" was released. It had a Southern plantation setting, Br'er Rabbit-type characters, and warm lovable real-life characters. The theme song is still indelibly etched in my mind. Music is good for the heart, and soul, and mind, and body. Life is better "With a Song in My Heart."

Music: vocal or instrumental sounds having rhythm, melody, or harmony; agreeable sounds (Merriam-Webster). One needn't sing nor play to enjoy music. One only needs to appreciate, to listen. Longfellow called music "the universal language of mankind." Think about the truth in that statement. "Music has charms to soothe a savage breast," claimed William Congreve, the English playwright.

Singing. Playing a musical instrument. Listening. How about the music of the birds? Maybe you can even whistle the tunes. It's all about appreciation. Our rural neighbors used to razz me in my youth about the various musical renditions they would hear above the sounds of our Farmall tractor. The long hours of fieldwork were better endured through singing or whistling. It was therapeutic. I'm especially advocating that type of music in this chapter, music that lifts you up by what it says as well as by how it sounds. The melodies help, of course, but it's the lyrics that I would covet for our lives. "With a Song...*in My Mind.*" It works both ways.

Some music builds up our confidence. Some music clears our consciences. Sometimes we just need music to escape. Young mothers-to-be often sing to the babies in their wombs. We have grandchildren who watch and listen to video tapes like "Baby Bach" and "Baby Mozart." How about leisure time music? Concerts, recitals, stereo, CDs, tapes. We listen at home, in the car, at the mall, in the dentist's chair, in the background of phone call-waiting services. Music, music, music.

Sing, hum, whistle, play, listen to music that's good for mind, body and soul. Be critical of your listening tastes as well as those of your loved ones. We can't travel to every place on earth, read every written word on earth, nor eat every edible on earth; therefore, be choosy. Do the same in music. Listen selectively. Why?

The headsets that abound around us and the radio stations that many are drawn to, especially our young people, are not all playing inspiring, edifying music! As you know, everything is available to our ears and minds these days. John Dryden reflected, "What passion cannot music raise and quell?" True. Oliver Hereford flippantly defined *song* as *"the licensed medium for bawling in public, things, too silly or sacred, to be uttered in ordinary speech."* Our moods and actions can be molded by what we hear. Even in its negative modes, it is a universal language. Make your listening constructive, not destructive, music.

We do have to choose, don't we? Classics, show tunes, sacred, gospel, big bands and swing, easy listening, jazz, rock and roll, hard rock, heavy metal, alternative, hip-hop, R and B, rap, country and blue grass, blues, solid gold, and hits of the decades. All the individual artists in all their various fields of music. You name it and the list goes on and on and on. There are innumerable options.

My musical tastes, probably like yours, vary with my needs. Heart, mind, body, and soul's needs. When I personally must have music the most, I try to nourish my soul. It encourages me. It reenforces me. Michael W. Smith's recent success, "Healing Rain," is a good example. As Thomas Carlyle said, music can be the "speech of the angels."

A prized gift that I received as a high school student was a book called *Living God's Way* by Rev. Reuben K. Youngdahl. It was a daily devotional and the following verse is from it. The verse is an endorsement of music as a safe harbor in our very challenging lives.

There's a song in my heart this morning; God placed its beauty there,
As He ushered in the eager dawn and found the time to share
A melody so precious, so cheerful, so divine;
It scattered all my anxious fears to heaven's holy clime.
How like the gracious Master who walks and talks with me
To send this sweet reminder that He wants my company!
That in His heavenly planning there's a song to lilt its way
Into each heart that listens...have you heard your song
Today?

Our overall philosophies may vary, but I would bet money that you do have those moments of needing "your song" too. I am recommending the following music because it has helped me through my ups and downs of life, when I was a teen, but also today. The songs are outlined on a Ten Rung Ladder. Life is a climb at times. Sometimes we require a ladder. The rungs represent various needs that we all have. There will be one or two example songs given in their entirety, followed by the titles of similar songs that you could find easily if you so desire. The songs are taken primarily from the *Lutheran Book of Worship*, Augsburg Fortress Publishing Company.

Select a rung that reflects your needs, moods, or mindset at a particular moment. Read from within that rung. Hopefully, on another day, you'll want to come back for more, the choices dependent upon your feelings at that time. These songs put us in the presence of some of the geniuses of music. The "speech of the angels" is truly stored in the archives of the centuries. This is the music of musicians who believed in a Supreme Being and a value system. These are the lyrics of people of faith. If you can hear the musical arrangements in your mind, hallelujah! If you aren't familiar with the melodies, you can easily track them down on tape, cassette, or CD. Most music stores will have a spiritual music category, and all religious music outlets will have renditions of songs such as these. Harmonies do richly support the lyrics, of course.

1st Rung: an A.M. Song

Morning Prayer

Father, we thank thee for the night...
and for the precious morning light,
for rest and food and loving care
and all that makes the world so fair.
Help us to do the things we should,
to be to others kind and good.
In all we do at work or play,
help us make this another blessed day.

2nd Rung: Faith

Kumbaya (Come by Here)

Kum ba ya, my Lord, Kum ba ya
Kum ba ya, my Lord, Kum ba ya
Kum ba ya, my Lord, Kum ba ya
Oh, Lord, Kum ba ya

Someone's crying, Lord, Kum ba ya
Someone's crying, Lord, Kum ba ya

Someone's crying, Lord, Kum ba ya
Oh, Lord, Kum ba ya

Someone's sleeping, Lord, Kum ba ya
Someone's sleeping, Lord, Kum ba ya
Someone's sleeping, Lord, Kum ba ya
Oh, Lord, Kum ba ya

Someone's singing, Lord, Kum ba ya
Someone's singing, Lord, Kum ba ya
Someone's singing, Lord, Kum ba ya
Oh, Lord, Kum ba ya

Also: My Faith Looks Up to Thee, #479
    Jesus, Priceless Treasure, #457
    Beneath the Cross of Jesus, #107
    Immortal, Invisible, God Only Wise, #526
    Were You There? #92

3rd Rung: Thanksgiving

This Is My Father's World, #554

1. This is my Father's world, And to my list'ning ears
   All nature sings, and round me rings The music of the spheres.
   This is my Father's world; I rest me in the thought
   Of rocks and trees, of...skies and seas; His hand the wonders
      wrought.

2. This is my Father's world; The birds their carols raise;
   The morning light, the lily white, Declare their maker's praise.
   This is my Father's world; He shines in all that's fair,
   In the rustling grass I...hear him pass; He speaks to me ev'rywhere.

3. This is my Father's world; Oh, let me not forget
   That though the wrong seems oft so strong, God is the ruler yet.

This is my Father's world; Why should my heart be sad?
The Lord is king, let the heavens ring; God reigns, let the earth
be...glad!

How Great Thou Art, #532

1. O Lord my God, when I in awesome wonder,
Consider all the worlds thy hand hath made,
I see the stars, I hear the rolling thunder,
Thy pow'r throughout the universe displayed;

CHORUS

Then sings my soul, my Savior God, to thee,
How great thou art! How great thou art!
Then sings my soul, my Savior God, to thee,
How great thou art! How great thou art!

2. When through the woods and forest glades I wander,
I hear the birds sing sweetly in the trees;
When I look down from lofty mountain grandeur
And hear the brook and feel the gentle breeze;

CHORUS

3. But when I think that God, his Son not sparing,
Sent him to die, I scarce can take it in,
that on the cross my burden gladly bearing
He bled and died to take away my sin;

CHORUS

4. When Christ shall come, with shout of acclamation,
And take me home, what joy shall fill my heart!

Then I shall bow in humble adoration
And there proclaim, "My God, how great thou art!"

CHORUS

Also: Beautiful Savior, #518
    My God, How Wonderful Thou Art, #524
    O Perfect Love, #287

4th Rung: Help

He Leadeth Me: Oh, Blessed Thought! #501

1. He leadeth me: oh, blessed thought!
   Oh, words with heav'nly comfort fraught!
   Whate'er I do, where'er I be,
   Still' 'tis God's hand that leadeth me.

CHORUS

He leadeth me, he leadeth me,
By his own hand he leadeth me.
His faithful foll'wer I would be,
For by his hand he leadeth me.

2. Sometimes mid scenes of deepest gloom,
   Sometimes where Eden's bowers bloom,
   By waters calm, o'er troubled sea,
   Still 'tis God's hand that leadeth me.

CHORUS

3. Lord, I would clasp thy hand in mine,
   Nor ever murmur nor repine;
   Content, whatever lot I see,
   Since 'tis my God that leadeth me.

CHORUS

4. And when my task on earth is done,
   When by thy grace the vict'ry's won,
   E'en death's cold wave I will not flee,
   Since God through Jordan leadeth me.

CHORUS

Also: O God Our Help in Ages Past, #320
     Let Us Break Bread Together, #212

5th Rung: Friendship

What a Friend We Have in Jesus, #439

1. What a friend we have in Jesus,
   All our sins and griefs to bear!
   What a privilege to carry Ev'rything to God in prayer!
   Oh, what peace we often forfeit;
   Oh, what needless pain we bear...
   All because we do not carry Ev'rything to God in prayer!

2. Have we trials and temptations?
   Is there trouble anywhere?
   We should never be discouraged...Take it to the Lord in prayer.
   Can we find a friend so faithful
   Who will all our sorrows share?
   Jesus knows our ev'ry weakness...Take it to the Lord in prayer.

3. Are we weak and heavy laden,
   Cumbered with a load of care?
   Precious Savior, still our refuge...Take it to the Lord in prayer.
   Do your friends despise, forsake you?
   Take it to the Lord in prayer.
   In his arms he'll take and shield you; You will find a solace there.

Living for Jesus

Living for Jesus, a life that is true.
Striving to please Him in all that I do
Yielding allegiance, glad hearted and free,
This is the pathway of blessing for me.

CHORUS

Oh, Jesus, Lord and Savior,
I give myself to Thee,
For Thou in Thy atonement
Didst give Thyself for me.
I own no other Master
My heart shall be Thy throne.
My life I give,
Henceforth to live,
Oh Christ, for Thee alone.

Living for Jesus Who died in my place,
Bearing on Calvary my sin and disgrace;
Such love constrains me to answer His call,
Follow His leading and give Him my all.

CHORUS

Living for Jesus through earth's little while,
My dearest treasure, the light of his smile.
Seeking the lost ones He died to redeem,
Bringing the weary to find rest in Him.

CHORUS

6th Rung: Warriors

Battle Hymn of the Republic, #332

1. Mine eyes have seen the glory of the coming of the Lord;
   He is trampling out the vintage where the grapes of wrath are stored;
   He has loosed the fateful lightning of his terrible swift sword:
   His truth is marching on.

CHORUS

Glory, glory! Hallelujah!
Glory, glory! Hallelujah!
Glory, glory! Hallelujah!
His truth is marching on.

2. He has sounded forth the trumpet that shall never call retreat;
   He is sifting out the hearts of men before his judgment seat.
   Oh, be swift, my soul, to answer Him; be jubilant, my feet!
   Our God is marching on.

CHORUS

3. In the beauty of the lilies Christ was born across the sea,
   With a glory in His bosom that transfigures you and me.
   As He died to make men holy, let us live to make men free,
   While God is marching on.

CHORUS

Also: A Mighty Fortress Is Our God, #228
    Onward, Christian Soldiers, #509
    Stand Up, Stand Up for Jesus, #389

7th Rung: Hope

Rock of Ages, Cleft for Me, #327

1. Rock of Ages, cleft for me, Let me hide myself in thee;
   Let the water and the blood, From thy riven side which flowed,
   Be of sin the double cure: Cleanse me from its guilt and pow'r.

2. Not the labors of my hands Can fulfill thy law's demands;
   Could my zeal no respite know, Could my tears forever flow,
   All for sin could not atone; Thou must save, and thou alone.

3. Nothing in my hand I bring; Simply to thy cross I cling,
   Naked, come to thee for dress; Helpless, look to thee for grace;
   Foul, I go to the fountain fly; Wash me, Savior, or I die.

4. While I draw this fleeting breath, When mine eyelids close in death,
   When I soar to worlds unknown, See thee on thy judgment throne,
   Rock of Ages, cleft for me, Let me hide myself in thee.

Also: Built on a Rock, #365

8th Rung: Service

Take My Life, That I May Be, #406

1. Take my life that I may be Consecrated, Lord, to thee;
   Take my moments and my days; Let them flow in ceaseless praise.

2. Take my hands and let them move At the impulse of thy love;
   Take my feet and let them be Swift and beautiful for thee.

3. Take my voice and let me sing Always, only, for my King;
   Take my lips and let them be Filled with messages from thee.

4. Take my silver and my gold, Not a mite would I withhold;
   Take my intellect, and use Ev'ry pow'r as thou shalt choose.

5. Take my will and make it thine; It shall be no longer mine.
   Take my heart, it is thine own; It shall be thy royal throne.

6. Take my love; my Lord, I pour At thy feet its treasure store;
   Take myself, and I will be Ever, only, all for thee.

O Master, Let Me Walk with You, #492

1. O Master, let me walk with you
   In lowly paths of service true;
   Tell me your secret; help me bear
   The strain of toil, the fret of care.

2. Help me the slow of heart to move
   By some clear, winning word of love;
   Teach me the wayward feet to stay,
   And guide them in the homeward way.

3. Teach me your patience; share with me
   A closer, dearer company,
   In work that keeps faith sweet and strong,
   In trust that triumphs over wrong,

4. In hope that sends a shining ray
   Far down the future's broad'ning way,
   In peace that only you can give;
   With you, O Master, let me live.

Also: Break Now the Bread of Life, #235

9th Rung: Peace

My Hope Is Built on Nothing Less, #293

1. My hope is built on nothing less
   Than Jesus' blood and righteousness;
   No merit of my own I claim,
   But wholly lean on Jesus' name.

CHORUS

On Christ, the solid rock, I stand;
All other ground is sinking sand,
All other ground is sinking sand.

2. When darkness veils his lovely face,
   I rest on his unchanging grace;
   In ev'ry high and stormy gale
   My anchor holds within the veil.

CHORUS

3. His oath, his covenant, his blood
   Sustain me in the raging flood;
   When all supports are washed away,
   He then is all my hope and stay.

CHORUS

4. When he shall come with trumpet sound,
   Oh, may I then in him be found,
   Clothed in his righteousness alone,
   Redeemed to stand before the throne!

CHORUS

Also: Peace, Like a River, #346
        Eternal Father, Strong to Save, #467

10th Rung: Songs for the Evening

Sun of My Soul, #77 (*Concordia Hymnal*)

1. Sun of my soul! Thou Savior dear,
   It is not night if Thou be near:
   Oh, may no earthborn cloud arise
   To hide Thee from Thy servant's eyes!

2. When the soft dews of kindly sleep,
   My weary eyelids gently steep,
   Be my last tho't how sweet to rest
   Forever on my Savior's breast!

3. Abide with me from morn till eve,
   For without Thee I cannot live;
   Abide with me when night is nigh,
   For without Thee I dare not die.

4. If some poor wand'ring child of Thine
   Have spurned today the voice divine,
   Now, Lord, the gracious work begin;
   Let him no more lie down in sin.

5. Watch by the sick; enrich the poor
   With blessings from Thy boundless store;
   Be every mourner's sleep tonight,
   Like infants' slumbers, pure and light.

6. Come near and bless us when we wake,
   Ere through the world our way we take,
   Till in the ocean of Thy love
   We lose ourselves in heaven above.

Abide with Me, #272

1. Abide with me, fast falls the even tide.
   The darkness deepens; Lord, with me abide.
   When other helpers fail and comforts flee,
   Help of the helpless, oh, abide with me.

2. I need thy presence ev'ry passing hour;
   What but thy grace can foil the tempter's pow'r?
   Who like thyself my guide and stay can be?
   Through cloud and sunshine, oh, abide with me.

3. Swift to its close ebbs out life's little day;
   Earth's joys grow dim, its glories pass away;
   Change and decay in all around I see;
   O thou who changest not, abide with me.

4. I fear no foe, with thee at hand to bless;
   Ills have no weight, and tears no bitterness.
   Where is death's sting? Where, grave, thy victory?
   I triumph still, if thou abide with me!

5. Hold thou thy cross before my closing eyes,
   Shine through the gloom, and point me to the skies;
   Heav'n's morning breaks, and earth's vain shadows flee;
   In life, in death, O Lord, abide with me.

Also: Now the Day is Over, #280

Through the highs and lows of my life, these songs have meant exactly what the rungs of the ladder suggest. They are indelible wrinkles on my mind which can be called up for support at any moment. The words give invaluable lessons and guidance. They give affirmation, assurance, and consolation. They generate focus whether skies are blue, black, or golden. Try them. I know the messages themselves will sustain you "when the going gets tough" and will uplift you "when the wind is at your back."

Music that stirs one's soul helps bring meaning, peace, and happiness to one's life. I sincerely believe it is good for you, me, and our world. It is good for our mental state as we work. Remember two things: (1) "Hi-Ho, Hi-Ho" is a great way to go to work! (2) "A man is born, but he's no good no-how, Without a Song!"

"*Dare to be strong and courageous.
Be brave enough to dare to be loved. Be Tandy.*"

- Sherwood Anderson

CHAPTER SIX

To Love and Be Loved

*I*n Richard Bach's book, *Jonathan Livingston Seagull*, Jonathan is taught the perfect invisible principle of life by Chiang, his elder. The principle is simple. If you become loving and give lovingly, you will be loved. A perfect principle? Certainly, to love and be loved is as close to perfection as we will ever get on this planet. An invisible principle? Invisible love is admirable, but visible love is admirable too. Let's examine love as a life inspired by acts of giving.

The Gift of Giving. My wife Mamie (her nickname) plants tiger lily seeds each spring. She waters and weeds her garden regularly. Her time is given freely and willingly. The expectations for the plants she's planted and the seeds she's sown have been far exceeded. Near her garden two cardinals daily alternate playing "look out" while their partner eats at the bird feeder. That is giving too. Gray mother squirrels bury butternuts in the same area for meals on winter's bad weather days. The young squirrels who mindlessly scramble their playful ways around the tree trunks while this is going on will be the benefactors. The gift of giving is present in all three of these examples. There is simple, honest, unselfish love in each of those acts.

I equate loving and giving to the ideas Bryan Doyle presents in an article entitled "Learning to Teach" from the July, 1996, issue of *Guideposts* magazine. Doyle conducts year-round baseball hitting clinics in Florida for young people.

"It was one of those days where it didn't seem to be sinking in. Staring at all those anxious, young faces, I realized the only hope I had of teaching effectively was to keep in mind how I had struggled to learn the game. I thought back to my father's indefatigable patience and how lovingly he had taught my brothers and me. Taking a deep breath and saying a silent prayer, I started over on the pivot spending as much time as necessary on each distinct element of the play."

A couple of key thoughts appear here: "lovingly taught" and "spending time." Love takes time and nurturing. Hasten slowly. Meaningful learning takes time. Giving takes time, but it reaps rich rewards.

The game of baseball truly is a great venue for learning with love. I work with those young faces of summer each year too, teaching six to eight-year old girls and boys how "to play ball." I tell our summer playground leaders to give praise as they teach. The youngsters must be "praised up." That's teaching with love. I say also, "You can never give them too many grounders, pop-ups, or swings. Each needed repetition is an adventure in learning for them." As in life, each act of love is a special adventure for both the giver and the receiver. Those receiving learn to love from being lovingly taught.

Spend meaningful time. Theologian Charles Swindoll says that seventy-five percent of being a successful minister is being available. I call that giving. Are you available for your spouse, your loved ones, your children? Are you available for your coworker, your neighbor, or for a struggling stranger who crosses your path? Maybe it's just to listen. Haven't we all needed that? Maybe listen and advise afterwards. Being available is meaningful caring. Giving one's time is an awesome gift. Giving is loving.

Several summers ago, a mother ape in a Chicago zoo picked up a three-year-old boy who fell into her cage. The mother thwarted off other apes who approached her as she carried the boy to a gate. What kind of an instinct is this? The ape saw someone in need and instinctually gave of herself to meet the need. Needless to say, this ape became the toast of the zookeepers and zoo-goers. In loving respect and material benefits, she received far more than she gave. An anonymous donor delivered fifty pounds of bananas to her for her actions. What was perfect was that she simply and unselfishly gave of herself to fulfill a need. She cared and she was unexpectedly blessed in return.

Now speaking of caring and being blessed, fellow Americans, we are "Part of the Main." Right? We aren't the only "Continent." True? Would you grant that destitute countries like Afghanistan, Uganda, Nigeria, Pakistan, and Cambodia are also "Part of the Main"? If so, what are we doing with all of our bountiful blessings, America? If we are honest, we have to admit we have received beyond belief. We do need to be more accountable for our "getting" and our "giving."

Moses, in the second book of the Bible says, "A tithe of everything from the land, whether grain from the soil or fruit from the trees, belongs to the Lord; it is holy to the Lord" (Leviticus 27:30 NIV). The tithe, as mentioned in Genesis 14:20 NIV, is one-tenth of one's assets. As a springboard for our sharing, giving, and caring, could we do more than just consider giving one-tenth of our good fortune to underprivileged people like those identified above? What would one-twentieth, to say nothing of one-tenth, do for our brothers and sisters in the family of man?

The tsunami flooding in the Far East resulted in approximately 220,000 deaths and 13 billion dollars of damages. Supposedly, one third of Americans donated to relief funds for victims. That is a step towards relating to our fellowman. More recently, Hurricane Katrina flooded America's Gulf Coast states. Eight hundred deaths. Damages may exceed 200 billion dollars. Again, American and world citizenry have responded remarkably. Why does it take natural disasters to arouse our compassion? We can't take it with us when we die. We could, and should, do so much more. We are "Part of the Main." We need to learn to give from our gifts. Just because we were born "here" and others were born "there" doesn't make us special! We are all "Family."

The true test will be whether we will take time to give and give again. Love isn't a one-time fling. Lovingly give, but also give again. The gift of giving. To lovingly practice this fundamental of life is to experience real living. If we do these things, the smiles of those who "have been loved," will be rewards for a lifetime. Take the time to give lovingly. It is the perfect principle. The giver always gets back. Luke in his New Testament description of Christ's Sermon on the Mount in Luke 6:38 NIV says, "Give, and it will be given to you. A good measure, pressed down, shaken together and running over, will be poured into your lap. For with the measure you use, it will be measured to you." America has received in great "measure."

St. Francis De Sales put it this way in an essay entitled, "Learning to Love":

Learning to Love

There are many who want me to tell them of secret ways of becoming perfect, and I can only tell them that the sole secret is a hearty love of God and the only way of attaining that love is by loving. You learn to speak by speaking, to study by studying, and just so, you learn to love God and man by loving. Begin as a mere apprentice and the very power of love will lead you on to become master of the art.

Oh, yes, to love and be loved! It is becoming on both the giver and the recipient!

Giving Perfectly. For many years my wife was a nurse for the elderly at the White Bear Lake Care Center. Among her Alzheimer's patients was a lady named Gladys whose response to almost any comment or happening was "That's perfect for me," usually accompanied by a shy smile and a bashful bowing of her head. Oh, that regardless of life's circumstances, we all could have Gladys' attitude. There can be perfection on earth, you know. Perfect is good!

We all crave perfection, but what is it really? The Merriam-Webster dictionary says it is "*being without fault or defect, the highest state of excellence.*" As I look straight overhead from my patio on a summer morning, I see the purest of beautiful blue skies. A very gentle cool breeze fans my skin. The squirrels play tag on a tree trunk. A male and female cardinal flit from tree to tree, getting closer to our house and the safflower-filled bird feeder suspended from the eaves. My wife's flower garden graces the backyard. Red and yellow roses, purple delphiniums, phlox, golden uros, marigolds, dahlias, and tiger lilies dot the scene. A butterfly or two or twelve and bumblebees visit the flowers and happily roam the garden. Look, feel, and smell. Without fault, the highest state of excellence. Perfection.

Bishop Jeremy Taylor defined love as "friendship set on fire." Express your friendship through love that genuinely cares and you will fan the flames. Singer and songwriter Michael W. Smith wrote, "Friends are friends forever." That is worth one's outreach of love, isn't it? And finally an anonymous writer once wrote "A friend is one who comes in when the whole world has gone out." Want friends? Want to love? Want to be loved? Be a friend. Reach out lovingly. Give perfectly.

What are some more examples of perfect love? You might anonymously leave a present for someone or just do a good deed for someone. Yes, Chiang and Jonathan, sometimes love is the perfect "invisible" principle. Going to your spouse's, girl friend's, or boy friend's place of work and leaving a surprise note, and maybe flowers or candy in his or her coat or in their work stations. I know that some of the finest moments of my life were the unexpected surprise gifts, thanks, or perks. It's the best. Please try it.

In *The Magnificent Obsession,* Bobby Merrick endures a tragedy and then undergoes a life-changing experience when he encounters a three-word philosophy of life: secretively, give generously. This is a work of fiction, but it has a Biblical basis in Matthew 6:1-4. Entertainer Carol Burnett benefited from this same philosophy when an unexpected benefactor gave her the funds to go to New York in search of work. She was financially incapable of this on her own. The only stipulation was that his name remain anonymous. The latter example is a career igniting success story from real life. In both cases, it worked out perfectly. Yes, this was "invisible" love.

However, sometimes love is the perfect "visible" principle too. Try bringing a casserole or some cookies to a neighbor. It is all the better if it's a neighbor you don't know well. Maybe they have just moved into your area. Giving some money to a charity that you believe in, but you've never actively supported. Loaning a stranger some change or a couple dollars when they're caught short-handed at a gas station or a sandwich shop. Giving is the missing component in many of our lives. Giving is perfect love, visible or invisible. Experience it. To love and be loved is where life is at.

One of the keys to a good family life is love. Sister Sledge's popular song says "We Are Family," meaning all of us are family. Remember, we are "Part of the Main," in the Far East, the Gulf Coast, or wherever. Loving the family of man means to freely and generously care for one another. Loving, caring, sharing, and giving of necessities, money, time, and talents to our fellowmen builds a world of confidence, hopes, and dreams. This is perfection in giving. Lives lived thusly become worthwhile. In fact, such a world is priceless. It is "family" to love.

The Stranger in "Tandy," a short story from Sherwood Anderson's novel, *Winesburg, Ohio*, comes to town and says, "I'm a lover and haven't found my thing to love." The Stranger came from a well-to-do family, but he has become an alcoholic. He comes to Winesburg in hopes of breaking his habit. Tom Hard and his five-year-old daughter become a sounding board for the Stranger. One night he tells them,

> "There is a woman coming. You may be the woman. They think it's easy to be a woman, to be loved, but I know better. I know about her struggles and her defeats. It is because of her defeats that she is to me the lovely one. Out of her defeats has been born a new quality in woman. I have a name for it. I call it Tandy. It is the quality of being strong to be loved. Be Tandy, little one. Dare to be strong and courageous. Be brave enough to dare to be loved. Be Tandy."

The Stranger is trying to give good counsel. The little girl never forgets him and begs to retain the nickname even after he has gone.

Our lives need courageous, strong people who are willing to give freely and generously. Mankind tends to be self-centered and selfish. Be brave enough to break from that and give to the "Family of Man." One can expect by expanding one's own territory to be loved in return. Is that scary? Come on. Don't let it be. Enjoy the excitement of giving. Dare to be Tandy. Dare to love and be loved. It's the perfect principle.

A Blueprint For Giving. Here's a four part blueprint for perfect love. First, acknowledge your fellowman on the street, on the elevator, in the peanut butter and jam aisle at the store, at the gas station, in an airport. Give a nod. Say "Hi" or "Hello." Smile, lighten up, warm up. Acknowledge that your companions on this road called life are alive too, are worthwhile too, and may be lonely, sad, happy, or loved too. The most stoic of them may most need your affirmations of their existences.

Second, reach out and touch someone. Yes, touch. I've had exchange students share with me how other cultures are so much freer to hug, kiss, or touch. We Americans have some ancestral inhibitions that we need to overcome. We also need some education as to the psychosexual implications of hospitality and salutation. Touching or hugging has no "implications" by anyone with good intentions! We have become paranoid about touching. We should not be crying "sexual harassment" if a friend or a stranger squeezes our hand, hugs our shoulders, or appropriately reaches out and touches us.

Liberty is not license. Reach out because you care. We aren't reaching out for cheap thrills. Touch because you are practicing the perfect, invisible, loving principle of life. I have needed a touch on a forearm, a hug around the shoulders, a hand clasp, a kiss. Haven't you? Samuel Johnson, the great English biographer, said figuratively of Oliver Goldsmith that he, "touched none that he did not adorn." By touching someone, you adorn that person's existence. You make a life better.

Third, help others. The storm has ended and your neighbor is sweating profusely while cutting, bundling, and hauling broken branches to the street. Volunteer some help. There's a car with a flat tire on the busy freeway's shoulder. Neither the driver nor the passenger perfectly exemplify "motor heads." Who will help? That big black Labrador from down the street is off his leash and playfully galloping through the neighborhood, overzealously flaunting his freedom at his owner. Then, there is the fresh, deep snowfall. There's really only one track in the street and sure enough, there's a car that slid on the curve and is stuck in the snow bank. If you stop in this depth, you may get stuck right in the middle of the street. Will you help? There are a multitude of needs that pass our horizons in a normal lifetime. "Do unto others what you'd appreciate having done to you." Love life and help out. It's a taste of perfection.

Finally, see a need and respond to it. Let me tell you of four philanthropists who filled dire needs. In 1998, Mark McGuire and Sammy Sosa both broke the all-time single-season homerun records. McGuire, the son of a southern Californian dentist, gives a million dollars a year to a child-abuse foundation. Sosa, a refugee who fled from the Dominican Republic at age 16, gives $500,000 a year to his homeland and recently purchased 250 computers for Dominican schools. See a need and fill it.

On the Minnesota baseball front, Hall-of-Famer Paul Molitor gives liberally to many causes, including a camp he opened in 1999 for children affected by AIDS. See needs. Respond to them.

Another humanitarian is Roger Swanson of White Bear Lake, Minnesota. A 3M engineer, he and his wife Thayle always had four to twelve foster children with disabilities in their home from the time I first knew him. At the same time, he'd be the first to volunteer weekly to feed the destitute at the Dorothy Day Center in St. Paul, one of many church activities in which he participates. Roger tragically passed away in early middle age. He was perpetually filling needs. He's immortalized in God's Hall of Fame.

Of course, we can't forget the ultimate love: sacrificial love, giving your life for another. As a boy, I marveled at the hen pheasant that would flatten herself to the ground over her nest of eggs in a heavily foliaged alfalfa field. The tractor and mower unknowingly approached. The farmer was oblivious until too late! Then, there is the legend about two friends who had been extremely faithful in helping each other. Suddenly, a ruthless tyrant seized their village and took one of the men as a hostage, condemning him to death. He pleaded to be spared temporarily so that he might say "good-bye" to his family and arrange for their safety. His plea was denied. It was then that his faithful friend came forward and made this promise: "Let me go for him. I will stay in prison and if he does not return, I will die in his place." The tyrant consented. The one man was set free and the other was put in chains. Sacrificial love.

The Bible speaks of this in St. John 15:13 NIV, "Greater love hath no man than this, that a man lay down his life for his friends." Sidney

Carton, in the climax to Charles Dickens' *A Tale of Two Cities*, heroically swaps places with a friend, Charles Darnay, and dies so that Charles can reunite with his fiance. Steven Spielberg's "Saving Private Ryan" does the modern day movie version of the same type of sacrificial love.

In conclusion let's listen to St. Francis of Assisi in his prayer perfect:

*P*rayer of St. Francis of Assisi

Lord, make me an instrument of your peace!
Where there is hatred, let me sow love;
Where there is injury, pardon;
Where there is doubt, faith;
Where there is despair, hope;
Where there is darkness, light;
Where there is sadness, joy.

To love and be loved, why, "Gladys, 'that's perfect for me,' too!"

Love Is An Enigma

One of the most beautiful aspects of life and yet also one of life's greatest mysteries is love. Phaedra, the step-mother in Euripides' Greek play *Hippolytus*, says to her nurse, "Ah, what is this strange thing that men call love?" Her nurse replies, "The sweetest thing in life, yet bitter too." How truly an enigma!

Love, endearment, devotion, adoration, fondness, affection, warmth, esteem, friendship, closeness, intimacy, attachment, regard, passion, infatuation, crush, enchantment, amour, ardor, rapture, desire, longing, sex. Is it as Ralph Waldo Emerson said, "Our highest word, and the synonym of God"? Or is it over-rated as Francis Bacon defined it, "A perpetual hyperbole." Love, affection, intimacy, passion, amour, desire, sex: the words do pique our interest, don't they? However, somewhere along the line, much of mankind has come to believe *love* only means *sex*. That is a mistake.

Sexuality is all around us. Modern society wants to titillate us with erotica. However, understanding that love is spiritual and intellectual as well as physical is the only bedrock for our understanding. The desire to be lovable and loved is not an excuse for the sex drive itself. Our lives may turn out to be favored with intimacy, passion, and sex, but the only love to count on is love that includes mind and spirit as well as the physical. In Galatians 5:16-17 NIV, Paul says, "So, I say, live by the Spirit, and you will not gratify the desires of the sinful nature." If you give lovingly of yourself to life and acquaintances, you most certainly will be lovable. As such, you will assuredly be loved in return. These are fundamental principles.

The *Oxford Dictionary of Quotations* has three hundred and thirty-one references for *love*. By contrast, the same book has twenty-five references for *sex*. If we could keep that approximate 10% proportion for the physical, I believe love would achieve the perfection that we all desire. If two are intellectually and spiritually "in love," the sexual instincts will naturally ensue. Focus on truly loving someone and being lovable, and the sexual attraction will probably follow.

> "Ah, Eros, Eros, whose hand distills
> Into our eyes the grace that fills
> With sweetness hearts Thou wouldst assail,
> Come not with evil on thy trail,
> Come not too wild!
> There is no star so blasting, fire so hot,
> As are the shafts that love hath shot,
> The Thunderer's Child."

This is the Chorus' proclamation in Euripides' play, *Hippolytus*. Eros, "Come not with evil on thy trail," sex *per se*. Come rather as a natural part of the passion of love.

Let's talk the bad news first. Society today is sex saturated! We're blitzed with electro-media sexsationalism: television soaps and talk shows, radio flippancy and irreverency towards sex, movies rated *R* to *X*, musical lyrics either directly or subliminally alluding to or blatantly flaunting sex, Internet "information," and provocative advertising to seduce all. Ethics and morality? Does society lack a moral consciousness? Is our insecure, immature, sexually bombarded world reflected in the rampant deviant behaviors of almost every day's news? Abuse, incest, pornography, kidnapping, rape, sodomy, perversion, distortion of natural male-female roles and actions. "Love? Bitter too, Phaedra?" That's an understatement!

Why do we so often abuse love? Is it a lack of a system of ethics? Is it a lack of moral fiber? Is it a lack of respect for God? Is it a lack of respect for mankind? Is it even a lack of respect for self?

Greece, the first great Western civilization, and the celebrated Roman Empire, the second hallmark Western civilization, both deteriorated from within. They broke down morally, ethically, and spiritually. America, is your love no more than, as Jonathan Benter put it, "an appetite placed in humans to insure breeding"? Will America be the third great Western civilization to rise and fall? Our modern-day society needs a soul-purging antidote of love: real, true love, "sweet love." Love of self, love of neighbor, love and respect of the opposite sex, and love of labor are connotations of "sweet love."

> *"Take a check-up*
> *From the neck up*
> *To eliminate stink'n think'n,*
> *And to prevent hardening of the attitude."*
>
> (Author Unknown)

It is never too late.

At this point we've reached the bottom of the barrel. It is the "half empty barrel," isn't it? Is it possible that there is another viewpoint? Is there any chance that the barrel is "half full" instead of "half empty"? I think so. Hopefully, the "sweetness" of this "strange thing called love" can overpower the "bitter."

Let us begin with the purely physical. Have you ever seen the *Venus de Milo,* even in pictures? Or how about Cellini's *Salt Cellar*? Rodin's *Adam*? *Girl Kneeling* by Maillol? These are beautiful classical sculptures, all made with the classical appreciation of the human body. Why are we at times embarrassed or uncomfortable about physical nakedness, natural physical beauty, or human sexuality? Why shouldn't we appreciate the beauty of the human body in sculptures, paintings, or in person? What a piece of work our bodies are! All the systems that they incorporate, none the least of which is our reproductive one! Why can't we hold those phenomena sacred? Embarrassed? We should rather be awe-struck by our sexuality, our attraction to each other, and our capacity to love and be lovable.

Understand this: all of us have our physicality and sexuality too. You and I need not be a male or female Greek sculpture on the facade of the

Mayo Clinic. But we all are lovable, attractive, and sexual if we want to be. If you want to be loved, you can become lovable. You need not be without love if a first or second love looks the other direction. There are many compatible partners available for all of us.

Myriad fish swim in the sea of humanity. Each has its beauty. Each is to be respected and loved. You just may be a tropical Jewelfish or a Neon Tetra. You are a work of natural art. You have your own attractiveness, sexuality, and sensuality. You have your own identity, your own love, and your own desire to be loved. You *will* be loved "sweetly." Give it time. Don't be embarrassed. Don't be obsessed. "Hasten slowly." Go as fast as you are comfortable while remaining in control of mind, body, and spirit. Give love, the perfect invisible principle, sanctity.

The Bible puts it this way in Genesis 2:18-25 NIV:

"The Lord God said, "It is not good for the man to be alone.
I will make a helper suitable for him! Now the Lord God
had formed out of the ground all the beasts of the field and
all the birds of the air...He brought them to the man to
see what he would name them; and whatever the man called
each living creature, that was its name. So the man gave
names to all the livestock, the birds of the air, and the beasts
of the field...But for Adam, no suitable helper was found.
So the Lord God caused the man to fall into a deep sleep;
and while he was sleeping he took one of the man's ribs and
closed up the place with flesh. Then the Lord God made a
woman from the rib he had taken out of the man, and he
brought her to the man. The man said, "This is now bone of
my bones and flesh of my flesh; she shall be called *woman*,
for she was taken out of man! For this reason a man will
leave his father and mother and be united to his wife, and
they will become one flesh. The man and his wife were both
naked, and they felt no shame."

Why should we?

Most certainly, "Hasten Slowly" on the sex. I guarantee it won't harm your "chosen one," you, nor your marriage, to say nothing of your possible children. Sexual intercourse: Leonard Levinson calls it "The formula by which one and one makes three." At age 21, 42, 63, whatever, what you anticipated, respected, and saved yourself for will be one of life's premier experiences. It is superlative. Save it for your special chosen partner for life. "Hasten Slowly." Premature use, and overuse, diminishes its value. It is priceless. Cherish the sanctity of your sexuality. "For this reason a man will be united to his wife and the two will become one flesh." Mind and body under control is the ideal speed for all of us.

Phaedra's nurse would rather have her lady and us experience, over and above anything else "the sweetest thing in life," *love*. Ralph Waldo Emerson, our great American essayist, called "*Love*: our highest word, the synonym of God." Novelist Pearl Buck explains, "Love cannot be forced, love cannot be coaxed and teased. It comes out of Heaven, unasked and unsought." Loving and being loved is sweet and lofty and heaven-sent. It is spiritual and intellectual as well as physical.

In her autobiography, *The Story of My Life*, Helen Keller tells how as a deaf and blind child she learned from Anne Sullivan the meaning of love.

A Child Learns About Love

"I remember the morning that I first asked the meaning of the word, 'love.' This was before I knew many words. I had found a few early violets in the garden and brought them to my teacher. She tried to kiss me; but at that time I did not like to have anyone kiss me except my mother. Miss Sullivan put her arm gently around me and spelled into my hand, 'Love, Helen.'

" 'What is love?' I asked.
"She drew me closer to her and said, 'It is here,' pointing to my

heart…her words puzzled me very much because I did not then understand anything unless I touched it.

"I smelled the violets in her hand and asked, half in words, half in signs, a question which meant, 'Is love the sweetness of flowers?'

" 'No,' said my teacher.

"Again I thought. The warm sun was shining on us.

" 'Is this not love?' I asked, pointing in the direction from which the heat came.…

"A day or two afterward…the sun had been under a cloud all day, and there had been brief showers, but suddenly the sun broke forth in all its southern splendor. Again I asked my teacher, 'Is this not love?'

"'Love is something like the clouds that were in the sky before the sun came out,' she replied. Then in simpler words than these, which at that time I could not have understood, she explained: 'You cannot touch the clouds, you know; but you feel the rain and know how glad the flowers and the thirsty earth are to have it after a hot day. You cannot touch love either; but you feel the sweetness that it pours into everything. Without love you would not be happy or want to play.'

"The beautiful truth burst upon my mind…I felt that these were invisible lines stretched between my spirit and the spirits of others."

Listen also to Antoine de Saint-Exupery's description, "Love does not consist in gazing at each other, but in looking together in the same direction." Love is intellectual, and spiritual, as well as physical.

Bodies without mind and soul are only physical and sexual. Bodies with mind and spirit are inner affirmations: Helen Keller's "invisible lines between spirits" and Saint-Exupery's "looking together in the same direction." The good news is that love means giving, both inwardly and outwardly. "Looking together" and "gazing at each other" may be synonymous with love: amazing, wonder-filled, wholesome, agape, perfect love.

Love is the perfect invisible principle. It means to generously give of one's self. However, being lovable and affectionate may not mean courtship, romance, marriage, and children. Regardless, love regenerates itself in the giver. Dare to love and give. You will get back.

Newell Edson's hallmarks of "genuine interest, greater happiness, feeling of comradeship, and pride in the other" are valid indicators of love at its best.

Hallmarks of True Love

A genuine interest in the other person and all that he or she says and does.

A community of tastes, ideals, and standards with no serious clashes.

A greater happiness in being with the one person than with any other.

A real unhappiness when the other person is absent.

A great feeling of comradeship.

A willingness to give and take.

A pride in the other person when comparisons are made.

Walter Rauschenbusch underscores the vitality and vigor of great love: "We never live so intensely as when we love strongly. We never realize ourselves so vividly as when we are in the full glow of love for others." Give greatly. Live greatly. Love greatly. Love physically, intellectually, and spiritually.

"Phaedra, we're focusing on the sweetness of love." Doesn't that sound good?

Wedding Day, 2005

Grover's Corner, USA

Dearly Beloved Wife or Husband,

Someone once defined love for me as "the genuine desire to share another person's downs and ups." Downs and ups are inevitable since we're humanly imperfect. If we realistically acknowledge both, I think we have a better chance to really love each other. Here's four suggestions for being good to your mate.

First, show your love. Frequently say "I love you," for example. You'll never say it too much. Say it at work and at play. Say it at dawn and at sunset. Say it by complimenting your partner's looks, actions, habits, insights, perseverance, efforts, etc. Any time is a good time for saying, "I love you." In addition, show your love. Show it by helping share the work load. Show it by doing more than your share. Also, love your partner by touching. Let your touch say, "I need you" just as it might say, "I love you." Being needed by your partner is a special kind of love. Say "I love you" with gifts and kindness: an opened door, a heartfelt thanks, an arm taken, a hand gripped.

"I love you" also connotes understanding, communication, and forgiveness. Love is sharing "down" times too. Air it out. Talk it out. Don't ever go to bed without communicating the issue. Don't ever be too proud to say "I'm sorry." Don't hide anything. Confront it. Talk...forgive...forget. It's critical to great love.

Second, learn through and about your marriage...the theory and reality. Read about successful marriages. Ask questions of people whom you respect for what you see in their relationships. Study parenting in the same way. Do recognize that in-laws are part of your relationship too. You didn't marry them, but they are part of your marriage's happiness or unhappiness. Learn as much as you can of theory. Then, cope effectively with reality.

Third, create time and space. Make time for each other. Not a cursory "How was your day?" but rather a genuinely interested question and "Quality Time" to hear the answer. We'd better be interested in the most important person in our lives, right? But, each of us needs space to meditate, to relax, to be independent too. Give your partner space whenever they want it. It is good for all.

Finally, season your love relationship with remembrances, surprises, and pizzazz. Remember anniversaries, birthdays, and any other significant times with gifts and celebration. Buy meaningfully. Plan a night out, even at a "new" place. Be very good at remembering. Also surprise your loved one. This might be the best symbol of your love. Use it. Go to your wife or husband's work place and leave a surprise gift. Leave a surprise love note where they're sure to find it. Do one of their daily tasks without them knowing it. On a day off, take them to a place they love to be or shop, give them $100 or the like and tell them you'll pick them up in five to eight hours. Get night-out eating reservations at a "special" place and tickets for an exceptional, cultural event. It's fun to surprise and be surprised.

When you got married, you most likely wanted your partner to be "full of fun" and "alive." Retain that into the second year of your marriage, as well as the twenty-second, and the forty-second. Try a variety of recreational, cultural, and social activities. There are so many. A summer picnic by a slow moving stream could be awesome. Keep the color and creativity in your marriage. Pizzazz means to be alive for each other. Be playful. Don't be afraid to tickle and tease. It's healthful. You're both individuals. Retain your winsome, original individuality. Have fun being alive and spirited. It keeps the pizzazz in your partnership.

I hope these ideas enrich your life and marriage.

Sincerely,

A Loved One

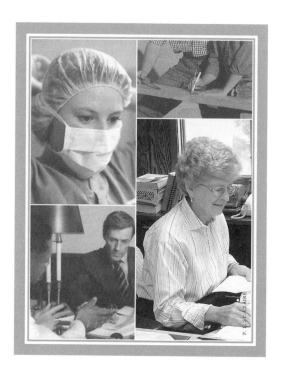

"For work is the grand elixer for all the maladies and miseries that ever beset mankind."

- Thomas Carlyle

CHAPTER SEVEN

To Work Is To Become

*S*t. Francis of Assisi was hoeing his garden when someone asked what he would do if he were suddenly to learn that he would die before sunset that very day. "I would finish my garden," he replied.

What or where is your garden...literally or figuratively? What is your labor of love? How much do you really love your work?

My wife loves to work in her flower garden. She takes pride in it: hoeing regularly, weeding by hand, lovingly watering, thinning out plants, trying new color combinations, adding new varieties to the landscape. Each spring and summer, she lovingly brings her best to her garden plot. It's her paradise, a veritable Garden of Eden. We, her family, appreciate the time, the energy, and the rewards she gets from her gardening. It's physically, mentally, and spiritually gratifying for her. This concurs with a recent report that gardening and home lawn care have become several of America's premier hobbies. Dorothy Gurney, in her poem "God's Garden," said:

The kiss of the sun for pardon,
The song of the birds for mirth,
One is nearer God's heart in a garden
Then anywhere else on earth.

My labor of love has been teaching high school English and coaching varsity high school sports. I slave at it, but I truly love it. Regardless of your line of work, we all need positive things, causes, purposes, tasks, labors, and gardens—places to invest our time and energies. The Roman philosopher Seneca called life, "A play. It's not in its length, but its performance that counts." A field of work wherein we wholeheartedly invest our time and energy is a high-performance life, a Pulitzer Prize-winning play.

Thomas Carlyle, the Scottish historian, philosopher, and author of *The Cure*, wrote:

The most unhappy of all men is the man who cannot tell what he is going to do, that has got no work cut out for him in the world, and does not go into any. For work is the grand elixir for all the maladies and miseries that ever beset mankind...honest work which you intend getting done.

I believe the creation of the world was an opportunity. That opportunity was abused and resulted in man's banishment from the Garden. "So the Lord God banished him from the Garden of Eden *to work the ground* from which he had been taken" (Genesis 3:23 NIV). To *work the ground*...what's your ground? What's your garden? What's your work? John Steinbeck's takeoff on this situation is a masterpiece. In his novel *East of Eden*, the land is the challenge that Caleb and Aron (like Cain and Abel, Adam and Eve's sons) must try to conquer.

Mankind had a blessed beginning in Paradise. Then, as a result of pride, man's sentence was to a life outside the Garden working the "soil." Spading, plowing, raking, planting, cultivating, and harvesting are basic constructive disciplines of the farming and gardening metaphor. The soil figure of speech represents lessons as to how to nurture, how to be involved in, how to live, and how to love life. Get down and dirty with some version of soil and work. Where are you working? What are you doing? Work is our grand commission.

We all need to experience work and its inherent ups and downs. There are great lessons in Mother Nature: sweat and tears, calluses and blisters, hammers and hoes. There are both scars and satisfactions as we work.

From the time of Creation in Genesis on to Steinbeck's symbolic version of the same story, mankind was placed east of Eden in order to learn from labor. James Montgomery defined it as "Labor, the symbol of man's punishment; Labor, the secret of man's happiness." What should I do when confronted with tough times in the work world? Charles, in Steinbeck's *East of Eden*, slavishly works the land. Charles and Adam are symbolically another pair of Cain and Abels. In prying a boulder loose in the field one day, the crowbar slips and clobbers him. The scar on his forehead is there for life. What should I do when psyched out, blistered, and scarred? How about inch by inch with the evergreen tree? Rev. Reuben Youngdahl in the book alluded to earlier described the phenomenon of the evergreen in this way:

After an exceptionally heavy snow storm, a father and his young son were out riding in an automobile. "Look at those elm trees," commented the father. "The branches are so badly broken that it is quite likely the trees will die. But now look at those evergreens. The snow hasn't damaged them at all." He continued, "There are two kinds of trees in the world...the stubborn and the wise. The elm tree holds its branches rigid and troubles pile on it until finally its limbs break, disfiguring the tree or killing it. But when the evergreen is loaded with more weight than it can hold, it simply relaxes, lowers its branches, and lets the burdens slip away. The evergreen is unharmed."

Relax, let go. Make like the evergreen.

Maybe the challenge is no job, or bummer jobs, or diabolic employers, or job lay-offs, and so on? What about cancer, Auschwitz, hurricanes, tornadoes, World War, Watergate, Presidential morals, my son's aneurysm, your family's calamity, theft, murder, rape? What about weeds in our gardens, boulders on our roads, and calamities in our lives? Depravity!

> Weeds: weeds come of themselves; flowers require cultivation. There is soil, a tendency to thorns and thistles. It is under the curse. Good things are brought out of the soil, like good things out of the human heart, only as the result of much labor. It takes no pain to produce a harvest of weeds, nor to produce the harvest that the thief or the drunkard reaps...no more effort than is required to float downstream. This is depravity.

> ("Gleanings for Sermons," Anonymous, *Leaves of Gold*)

There is an interesting anecdote about John Ruskin, the art critic, as he practiced Robert Schuller's "Scars into Stars" philosophy. A young woman relative of his had been given a beautiful silk handkerchief by a friend. Accidentally, she overturned a bottle of ink on it and spoiled a good part of it. She felt very bad as she thought of this beautiful gift being ruined by her own carelessness. Ruskin came into the room and saw her distress. Smiling he took the handkerchief from her. When he returned, she couldn't believe it was the same handkerchief. "Yes, it's yours," he said, "I simply took the ugly blot and transformed it into a picture." We should all adapt so well to our soiled-spoiled blots, to our scars, and to our challenges . Robert Burns, the Scottish poet, in his poem, "To A Mouse," puts it this way, "The best laid schemes o 'mice an' men gang oft a-gley." Our best laid plans often go awry. What we do then is how we should be measured.

Remember, "the land" is a metaphor for a place to develop good work habits and responsibility. Meaningful, challenging work is the bottom line. As Voltaire reminds us in *Candide*, "We must cultivate our garden." An anonymous poet describes it this way:

I Am Work

> *I am the foundation of all business.*
> *I am the source of all prosperity.*
> *I am the parent of genius.*
> *I am the salt that gives life its savor.*
> *I am the foundation of every fortune.*
> *I can do more to advance youth than his own parents,*
> *Be they ever so wealthy.*
> *I must be loved before I can bestow my greatest blessings*
> *And achieve my greatest ends.*
> *Loved, I make life sweet, purposeful, and fruitful.*
> *I am represented in the humblest savings, in the largest*
> *Block of investments.*
> *All progress springs from me.*

To truly live is to have purpose. A work of love, a land to cultivate, gives us opportunity and purpose. H.W. Prentis, Jr., in "Your Best Foot Forward," put it this way:

"Which sounds longer to you…569,400 hours or 65 years? They are exactly the same in length of time. The average man spends his first 18 years…157,000 hours…getting an education. That leaves him 412,000 hours from age 18 to 65. Eight hours of every day are spent in sleeping; eight hours in eating and recreation. So there is left eight hours to work in each day. One-third of 412,000 hours is 134,000 hours…the number of hours a man has in which to work between the age of 18 and 65. Expressed in hours, it doesn't seem a very long time, does it? Now I am not recommending that you tick off the hours that you worked, 134,000, 133,999, 133,998, etc., but I do suggest that whatever you do, you do it with all that you have in you. If you're sleeping, sleep well. If you're playing, play well. If you're working, give the best that is in you, remembering that in the last analysis, the real satisfactions in life come not merely from money and things, but from the realization of a job well done. Therein lies the difference between the journeyman worker and a real craftsman."

Be a craftsman. Do it well, whatever you choose to do. There are endless possibilities for work. That's good for we are all individuals with a wide variety of interests. There are "different strokes for different folks." John Banister Tobb's short poem, "The Sisters," exemplifies the importance of different worthwhile works.

> The waves forever move;
> The hills forever rest:
> Yet each the heavens approve,
> And love alike hath blessed
> A Martha's household care,
> A Mary's cloistered prayer.

Different involvements for different personalities? Sure. Different occupations, recreations, and work? Good. Be involved. Work, sweat, be fruitful, enjoy, but work. If it's purposeful labor, the rewards will be gratifying and healthy. Remember the words of the heart surgeon: "If you don't sweat every forty-eight hours, I'll probably be making an incision in your chest cavity because of your clogged, corroded arterial plumbing!" Sweat can have tremendous rewards, for today and for tomorrow.

When I labor, I sweat. When I'm sweaty, I lose my inhibitions. I'm real. I'm genuine. All pretenses get washed away. The drenched creature is the real me. There is no bravado to being soaking wet from rain or sweat. If I can love my work, I'm free to be that real me. Diligent work frees me to be a credit to my labors, to my loved ones, and to society.

These are my premises. First, appreciate the opportunity to work. Second, lovingly give your best to your work. It will satisfy. It will free you. Dick Proenneke has lived in the hinterlands of Alaska, his "Wilderness Wonderland," for 30 years. This 82-year-old pioneer loves this "nice place" among the grizzly bears, moose, caribou, Dall sheep, lake trout, Dolly Varden, and Grayling. He built his home (a 12 x 16 cabin) in 3 months at a cost of $10. He went there to find "if I was equal to everything this wild land could throw at me." As Henry Thoreau of Walden Pond, a century earlier, said, "I went to the woods because I wished to live deliberately, to front only the essential facts of life." These men loved their work and their places to work.

A positive work ethic appears in sources as diverse as Henry David Thoreau, Andrew Lloyd Weber, *Porgy and Bess*, and children's songs. "Hi-Ho, Hi-Ho, It's off to work we go." Can you "whistle while you work"? It is therapeutic. "I've been working on the railroad, all the live-long day. I've been working on the railroad, just to pass the time away." I hear a positive work ethic in "Old Man River," too: "You and I, we sweat and strain, fightin' and trouble are our middle names.....but, Old Man River, he just keeps rollin' (paraphrase: keeps workin'), he keeps on rollin' (workin') along." Whistle at work. Master your soil. Fill your day with meaningful work. Keep on "rollin'."

I want to live and work so when I die, it's a happy funeral. Consider my former principal and athletic director, Roy Wahlberg, who enriched every endeavor he attempted. Consider the foster mother who takes in seventeen children as her daily challenge. Consider the elderly Sunday school teacher who keeps on humbly giving to youngsters even though she's 70. Consider the professor who continues to teach despite the inconvenience of a wheelchair. These are good, full lives well-lived. Work that is meaningful and isn't self-centered is good work. Work that benefits society is always good work. I'd like a good-feeling funeral. How about you?

Stephen Grellet's exhorted us in the Prologue:

> I expect to pass through this world but once;
> Any good thing therefore that I can do,
> Or any kindness that I can show to any fellow-creature,
> Let me do it now;
> Let me not defer or neglect it,
> For I shall not pass this way again."

R.L. Sharpe, the 19th century poet, wrote of what we have to bring to our work:

A Bag of Tools

Isn't it strange
That princes and kings,
And clowns that caper
In sawdust rings,

And common people
Like you and me
Are builders for eternity?

Each is given a bag of tools,
A shapeless mass,
A book of rules;
And each must make,
Ere life is flown,
A stumbling block
Or a stepping stone.

Wouldn't the world be better off if more of us were stepping stones?

"Work is love made visible" said Kahil Gibran, in his work *The Prophet*. Karel Capek wrote, "There was something good in service and something great in humility. There was some kind of virtue in toil and weariness." John Ruskin, the English writer and art critic referred to earlier, reflected on work by writing, "The highest reward for a man's toil is not what he gets for it, but what he becomes by it." Aha, to work is to become! To seek and accept work as a fundamental part of life is to spawn energy for both mind and body. The power of becoming.

"*Am I a builder who works with care,*
Measuring life by rule and square?
Am I shaping my deeds to a well-made plan,
Patiently doing the best I can...
Or am I a wrecker who walks the town
Content with the labor of tearing down?"

- Anonymous

CHAPTER EIGHT

What Work?

*W*ork is the life-blood of meaningful existence. What type of work then makes for a good life? How about a garden to hoe? A song to write? A plane to fly?

How do we find the answers as to what work is best for us? Begin with prayer. Maybe we have to do stop-gap work to pay the bills while we pray, but continue to pray. Pray for meaningful work at which you can be productive. There is an old German quotation, "Do you pray as though no work will help and work as though no prayer will help?" Prayer is a basic tenet of life, a common denominator that we all need to function from in our world. If presently, you do not buy that, I ask you to re-examine your reasoning.

Let me give an example. With all due respects to the surgeon Dr. Michael Madison, and the chief neurologist Dr. Paul Schanfield, I believe my thirty-four year old son would not have recovered from four operations and a total of fifteen hours of brain surgery for an aneurysm without the prayers of friends from Minnesota to Texas to Alaska to

Africa. Men, the specialists, were excellent at their work. God, answering a multitude of prayers, was awesome. Perhaps prayers from a doctor and a neurologist too.

What should I pray? How specifically do I pray? Do I pray for the perfect work for me? Do I dare pray for the ideal life partner? Why not? The most important issues of one's life—spouse, children, jobs, troubles, illnesses—are fit material for us to pray about. If I pray in faith, issues both large and small will be resolved in God's good time. That's a leap of faith. Ask and then listen. Jesus said in Matthew 17:20 NIV, "I tell you the truth, if you have faith as small as a mustard seed, you can say to this mountain, 'Move from here to there' and it will move. Nothing will be impossible for you."

Another fundamental: talk things over with your Lord as early in the day as you can. As the song insinuates, there will be a daily "blessed assurance" that you aren't going out into that challenging world of ours alone. Mankind, no matter how big he or she is, needs to talk to a Higher Authority to live a productive day. This is a key for identifying what work to do. We need to ask for guidance in order to come to understanding. Ask, listen, and then thank.

The contemporary baseball movie, *Field of Dreams*, coined the expression, "If you build it, they will come." Dreams brought to fruition. Kevin Kostner's baseball field from a cornfield. Frank Lloyd Wright's awe-inspiring architecture. Space travel resulting in moon landings. Rev. Robert Schuller's dream evolving from drive-in theater to Crystal Cathedral in Garden Grove, California. Flight from the "other" Wrights, Wilbur and Orville! Dreams foreseen do materialize. Walt Disney once remarked, "If you can dream it, you can do it. Remember this whole thing was started with a dream and a mouse." I believe it. Be confident.

Please be patient after you pray and dream about your work. We serve even in those stop-gap jobs by being patient. John Milton, blind at age forty-four, exemplified patience. In a sonnet "On His

Blindness," he concludes, "They also serve who stand and wait." Twenty years later he had completed *Paradise Lost* and *Paradise Regained*, two of the world's classics of literature. Even if you aren't suffering as he was, heed Milton's words. Be patient.

Robert Schuller's axiom for patience was mentioned earlier: "Inch by inch, everything's a cinch. Yard by yard, everything is hard." Ask earnestly and wait for an answer. Meanwhile, "As long as it is day, we must do the work of Him who sent me. Night is coming when no one can work" (John 9:4 NIV). This may be the stop-gap, pay-the-bills job holding. Be patient. I mentioned early in this book a treasured coaster that has this tranquil little country scene and the words "Bloom where planted" imprinted on it. Patience. Savor the moment wherever and whatever the work.

Work and appreciate the work opportunities that come your way. Appreciate the half-full glass over the half-empty glass. Small jobs, part-time jobs, dual jobs, even the littlest jobs. Be thankful for any type of work. The work itself and the inherent sweat are the labors of love east of Eden. Appreciate the yards and the inches, the mountains and the valleys, the eagle and the sparrow en route. Appreciate the chance for work itself until that "dream" job, or at least that "better" job comes along. Give them all your best. Appreciate them.

John Ruskin, the English writer mentioned earlier, reflects on work in this way:

"In order that people may be happy in their work, these three things are needed: they must be fit for it; they must not do too much of it; and they must have a sense of success in it—not a doubtful sense, such as needs some testimony of other people for its confirmation, but a sure sense, or rather knowledge, that so much work has been done well and fruitfully done, whatever the world may say or think about it."

Rudyard Kipling agrees. "The only thing a man can do is paint the best canvas he can, hang it out between the bamboo trees to dry, and then let the monkeys come around to criticize."

"Am I fit for this work?" I want to be a pilot, but my eyes are 20/80. I want to be a world-class sprinter, but my 100 meters time is 12.1. I want to be a scientist or mathematician, but my forte is the arts or the humanities. "Am I fit?" is critical. Dreams, yes, but with realistic hopes of attainment. "If your mind can perceive, If your heart can believe, If your hands can achieve"—then you're fit for this work. To be happy in our fields of work we must be fit for them.

What kind of work shall I do? Omaha Bee speaks of coming to understand what work we should do in her essay, "Building Cathedrals."

Building Cathedrals

Three men, all engaged at the same employment, were asked what they were doing. One said he was making five dollars a day. Another replied that he was cutting stone. The third said he was building a cathedral. The difference was not in what they were actually doing, although the spirit of the third might quite possibly have made him the more expert at his task. They were all earning the same wage; they were all cutting stone; but only one held it in his mind that he was helping build a great edifice. Life meant more to him than to his mates, because he saw further and more clearly. The farmer may be only planting seed, but if he opens his eyes he is feeding the world. The railroad man, the factory hand, the clerk in the store, likewise are building their cathedrals. The investors in stocks and bonds, the executives of great corporations…they are building cathedrals likewise, if only they can catch the vision. The housewife does not count the dollars she receives for her exertions. If she did, her life would be unhappy indeed. The rest of us, the great figures of the industrial world more than the humbles ones, are thinking too much about such things as cutting stone, and making profits, fully to be realizing the beauty of life.

Are you and I just making money through our work? Are we just putting in our time on work shifts? Or are we building edifices? If I'm fit to be a builder, if I fit my craftsman's role, then, I'm an architect, a designer, an inventor, an engineer, and a creator of cathedrals. These edifices bring happiness to others and to me. Are you fit for building cathedrals? Good questions.

Ruskin's second premise for a happy work life was, "Don't do too much of your work." Don't become stale. Don't burn out. Familiarity breeds contempt is the axiom. Solomon spoke of moderation in all things, even in work. Break or vary the routine of your work and day. Take a vacation. Try a new eating spot and some new foods. Dare to be innovative. Take calculated risks. Don't perpetually take your work home. Assuredly, there's work to be done, but hasten slowly. Go as fast as you can and yet be under control.

Finally, Ruskin knows that we need to feel successful at what we're doing in order to be happy in our work. Humanity needs challenges. Humanity needs to have success meeting challenges. We need work that tests our capabilities. We need work that we can take pride in when finished. I like the medieval idea of challenges. They called them quests: quests for the Holy Grail, Arthurian quests. I liked quest activities in the classroom too. Challenges for the students to identify and conquer.

Our work needs quests. Something to strive for, to reach for, and to live for. However, quests do need to be attainable. In quest of the best looking classic car in town, in quest of the best landscape on the street, in quest of the Betty Crocker homemaker award, in quest of daily bread, in quest of shelter and clothing, in quest of $10,000, in quest of a record. Challenges are stimulating, even the recreational ones like puzzles, wire rings, mind games, "Who-done-its?" Challenges give stimulus to our work. That is both healthful and productive. If creativity, which we all have, can be tapped to meet a challenge, it is especially satisfying work. Seek work that challenges your abilities and yet gives you a chance to succeed. This is personal satisfaction.

Whatever type of work eventually comes your way, large or small, make it your masterpiece. You will never regret that type of artistry to your day. And when your best efforts do merit the "plaudits of the throngs," stay humble. Consider Albert Einstein's equation: "If A is a success in life, then A equals X plus Y, plus Z. Work is X; Y is play; and Z is keeping your mouth shut." (*Observer* 15, January, 1950). Consider Odysseus and his mouth problems. He's vain and proud. The gods, especially Poseidon, God of the Sea, decided that he could use some humility. Odysseus must labor through a host of Spartan challenges over ten years of time before he's "allowed" to return home. Quite simply, it is Einstein's Z in the equation of successful living: "Keep your mouth shut." It's a fine equation. Be humble. Be thankful.

Or ask the hero of Leo Tolstoy's s short story "How Much Land Does a Man Need?" The hero is told by God that he can have all the land that he can navigate on foot from sunrise to sunset. However, he must be back to the starting point by sunset. Of course, vanity and pride overextend his aspirations, and trying to return to the starting point by evening, he collapses and dies from total physical exhaustion with the starting point within eyesight. Six feet of ground to be buried in is "all the land a man needs!" Tolstoy has a good point. Be humble in your labors, even the extremely enticing ones.

A key closing question is posed by an anonymous poet.

Builder or Wrecker

I watched them tearing a building down,
A gang of men in a busy town;
With a ho-heave-ho and a lusty yell,
They swung a beam and the side wall fell.
I asked the foreman: "Are these men skilled?
And the men you'd hire if you had to build?"
He gave a laugh and said, "No indeed...
Just common labor is all I need.
I can easily wreck in a day or two
What builders have taken years to do."

And I thought to myself as I went my way,
Which of these roles have I tried to play?
Am I a builder who works with care,
Measuring life by rule and square?
Am I shaping my deeds to a well-made plan,
Patiently doing the best I can...
Or am I a wrecker who walks the town
Content with the labor of tearing down?

We need more builders. Builders rule. They rule in work and life. They optimistically live each day to the fullest. Work, play, and be humble.

The poem below by Henry Van Dyke gives the ultimate attitude in regards to whatever work comes our way.

Work

Let me do my work from day to day.
In field or forest, at the desk or loom,
In roaring marketplace or tranquil room;
Let me but find it in my heart to say
When vagrant wishes beckon me astray:
"This is my work; my blessing, not my doom;
of all who live, I am the one by whom
this work can best be done in the right way."

Then shall I see it not too great, nor small
To suit my spirit and to prove my powers;
Then shall I cheerful greet the laboring hours,
And cheerful turn when the long shadows fall
At eventide, to play and love and rest,
Because I know for me my work is best.

Work gives meaning to my day. Not being afraid to work is a mark of strength, not weakness. To carry your share of the load is to really become. And remember, no one ever drowned in sweat. Work gives purpose to life. To have purpose is to be at peace with one's world. Work is good.

Labor Day, 2005

Industrial City, USA

Dear Custodial Engineers (Workers of the World):

"I've got two vital principles for you," said my first teaching mentor. "One, don't lose your keys. Two, the custodians are just as important as the teachers, principals, or superintendent. Treat them right." I hope I have. I know you deserve more than I've given back to you. You are the mortar that holds schools, offices, and businesses together. I write this letter to custodial engineers, but it applies to all service workers and manual laborers.

Thank you so much for all you do. Lift, unload, unpack, move. Clean, clean, clean. Gum, garbage, "chew," pop, candy...and toilets! Remember to smile!! Take care of the physical premises: the cafeteria, the classrooms, the hallways, and the immediate exterior of the building and grounds. The blackboards, the grease boards, the carpet, the tile, the thermostats, the furniture, the locker rooms, the gymnasiums, and so on. Of course, it's understood that the preparations for all of these happenings will be "on time." Bad public relations otherwise. Be especially immaculate for Open House, parent-teacher conferences, choir and band concerts, games, and "special" events. Obviously, don't get sick, for goodness sake, or our spotless "image" could be tarnished. And, remember again, smile.

You are caretakers, guardians, conservators, janitors, keepers, maintenance experts, stewards, watchmen, curators, engineers, and sometimes psychologists and counselors. You are Jacks-and-Jills-of-all-trades.

Thank you so much for your service. Thank you for all that you do. You do make the difference. You are appreciated. "Mortar?" You bet! "As important as anyone here?" You better believe it!

Teddy Roosevelt said, "The credit belongs to the man who is actually in the arena, whose face is marred with dust and sweat." That's you, guys and gals. I'm proud to have worked with you. Do you remember the quote, "They also serve who stand and wait?" I've got a paraphrase tribute for you: "They also serve who kneel and scour!" Let none of us forget it.

Best Wishes,

A Co-Worker

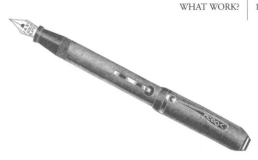

12th of Always

ala M.I.T., USA

Dear Professionals,

The Merriam-Webster dictionary defines professional as *"a calling requiring specialized knowledge and often long academic preparation."* You are "an expert, a master, an old hand, a virtuoso" then. You are skilled and proficient. Plumber, car mechanic, electrician, teacher, coach, lawyer, doctor...that's you...schooled, trained, accredited...and, yes, experienced. The pro does go into the field for his or her apprenticeship. The experience seasons one for the professional challenges.

This letter is about what I've learned from being a professional employee and from hiring professional employees.

First of all, a professional should be confident. Your training, knowledge, and experience should enable you to act with assurance: to be positive and decisive as you perform your duties. Believe in yourself. If you prepared well, you can act with certainty.

A related characteristic is pride. A pro prides himself in his craft, his work. It's related to self-confidence. It has been referred to as subtle arrogance: "I know I'm good and because of that I will do well." With this pride, good performance is expected.

Next, if I work for you or you work for me, I'd like to have us love what we do. Seek challenging and rewarding work. A professional who loves his work will work well. Realistically, some may have to love the people or the environment where they work, over and above the work they do. That works too. Love those co-workers. Love the climate of the workshop.

If Abe Burrows is right that "Love is when another person's needs are as important as your own," then strive to serve through your work. If my painting your interior walls or my salesmanship of family room furniture to you brings happiness to you, haven't I served? My lifetime experience has taught me that when I give lovingly, I get in return. Many professional opportunities will directly involve service. If it isn't inherent to your work, then seek service opportunities in your free time by volunteering. Such giving will energize you because it's an act of love.

Sir Cecil Spring-Rice wrote a patriotic poem, "I Vow to Thee, My Country." I think we can parody the title and first line, and it will be appropriate for this letter.

> I vow to thee, my profession...all earthly things above...
> Entire and whole and perfect, the service of my love,
> The love that asks no question: the love that stands the test,
> That lays upon the altar the dearest and the best:
> The love that never falters, the love that pays the price,
> The love that makes undaunted the final sacrifice.

Oh, that all our professional work reflects such love and sacrifice.

Now, maybe there are some professionals who are totally independent or autonomous. In which case, do remember again, John Donne's words, "No man is an island entire of itself, every man is a piece of the Continent." Somewhere, somehow, we are serving humanity as professionals. We all are part of the continent. Be loyal. The ultimate unit is a team of "We and Us" people, not "Me and My" professional agendas.

Given the above characteristics, my professional friend, quality work should be the subsequent trademarks of our efforts. To paraphrase Hallmark cards, "We cared enough to do our very professional best." We put in the time, the extra hours. When I coached, we always gave the captains of our teams a brief creed to lead by: "Be the first on the practice or game field or floor, and be the last to leave." It will never diminish your vocational excellence either.

Quality work will also embody problem solving, I believe. The master professional can creatively solve challenges if his book knowledge is insufficient. If he doesn't know quite enough, he does know how to find the answers. Quality work will be done. "I will leave the given situation better than I found it."

Also, exercise will power. Coach Jon Chaney of Temple University constantly reminds his athletes, "Your will is greater than your skill." Hunger, thirst, long, ache for professional success and you will achieve it. Mind over matter. Mental above physical. Heart. Undying willpower guarantees professional success.

Last, make this your professional motto: "Quality, excellence, distinction, caliber, and class." Good luck.

Sincerely,

A Fellow Pro

P.S. I watched an ultimate professional referee, Ed Rush, officiate a NBA game recently. With confidence, he made his calls. With humor and compassion, he listened to both players' and coaches' complaints. With personality, he schmoozed with the fans at timeouts. He looked, acted, and performed as a man proud of his trade. Go and do likewise.

"*If I had my life to live over, I would start barefooted in the spring and stay that way later in the fall. I would play hooky more. I wouldn't make such good grades except by accident. I would ride on more merry-go-rounds. I'd pick more daisies.*"

- Anonymous

CHAPTER NINE

Little Things Mean A Lot!

*L*ittle things are omnipresent. In combination, the little things are the substance of the big things in life. They may make or break a team, a marriage, a business, or a corporation. Cells, atoms, neutrons, microcosms: they may soon constitute the body, the bomb, the nuclear energy, the macrocosm. From tiny acorns, huge oaks grow. From minuscule snowflakes, giant snow banks burgeon. What we consider unimportant may well have great significance. As a popular song by Joni James reminds us, "Little Things Mean A Lot."

> "Blow me a kiss from across the room,
> Say I look nice when I'm not,
> Touch my hair as you pass my chair,
> Little things mean a lot."
>
> (lyrics by Carl Stutz)

Thomas Edison, who patented 1,100 inventions in sixty years, had innumerable failures with the electric light until he placed a filament of carbonized thread in a bulb. He had needed something that did not contain air, like ordinary cotton sewing thread burned to an ash. A little thing with an enormous impact.

A faucet leak as tiny as a pin prick results in a loss of 62,000 gallons of water in a year. Little things.

The scoreboard favored us 55-52 with 6.1 seconds left in regulation time. Our opponent was shooting two free throws. The shooter made the first, 55-53, but the second shot dropped short and... bounced back toward him. Two of our players were talking to each other as the shot left his hand, and stood mesmerized at the side of the lane as the shooter followed his shot and scored to send the game into overtime. Blocking out is a fundamental little thing. We lost in overtime.

How about the job interview with an abundance of qualified candidates? One of the applicants worked faithfully for two years under the supervisor's old college friend in another city. Little things.

I maintain that we need to see the nearby as well as the far out, the fireflies as much as the fireworks. We need to move at a pace that allows us to value and respect the world around us. We need to slow down, drink in, appreciate, and be sensitive to the little things.

We've all seen little boys and girls running over lawn sprinklers and being "goosed-thrilled" in each passage. How about the ladies with arms loaded with shopping bags? Freedom to shop, even for "little things." Holidays are few out of a total of 365 days, but little breaks like Valentine's Day, Easter, 4th of July, Halloween, Thanksgiving, and Christmas are big in significance.

How about appreciation? Do you appreciate your bed? Do you appreciate that driver on the street or highway behind you who is patient enough not to tailgate or, after passing you, doesn't cut back in on you the minute he's one car length ahead? Do you appreciate the reservoir of your mind, your storehouse computer? How about those creeds of your childhood and youth which are forever buried there? Maybe it's the 23rd Psalm, or a Boy Scout creed, or the "Seize the day" slogan of the *Dead Poets' Society*, or the Lord's Prayer. Or how about those song lyrics from the past?

Appreciation. How did you feel when you received an unexpected thank-you note? How did you feel when you wrote that thank-you note? Thank-you notes, personal letters, E-mail, or whatever: there are psychological by-products of mail. Have you observed the body language of people going to their mailboxes and opening them? "No mail today? Oh!" Our responses often symbolize the "nobody loves me" concept. Mail is related to love. Someone cared enough to try to communicate with us.

The same applies to oral communication. Did you ever smilingly say "Hi," "Hello," or "Good Day to You," to a stranger you passed in a skyway, stood by in an elevator, or encountered in a store? Didn't you usually receive an affirmation in return? How do you feel when someone, friend or stranger, waves at you? Isn't it good to be recognized? Don't you simultaneously want to acknowledge them? As Ralph Waldo Emerson said, "It's never too soon for a kindness because you never know how soon it might be too late." Little things give meaning to the moment. "Bloom where you are planted."

How about the natural world? What do you see? A beautiful, soft, pink amaryllis is growing an inch a day in front of your picture window. A rainbow after a summer shower. A red-orange sky at sunset. The diamond-like sparkle of the moon. Lights reflecting on newly fallen snow. The warmth of the sun on your body on a perfect summer day. The comfort of a shade tree when the sun becomes too intense. Gentle, warm, caressing rain. Little, natural phenomena.

Devoted pets. A purple ribbon Grand Champion Aberdeen Angus heifer. A 200 pound Chester White who contentedly lets a 10-year-old sleep on his warm belly during a noisy night at the State Fair. Buster,

Mitzi, Morgan, Kenai, Anya, Lily: what's more faithful than one's dog? ? I love to watch a dog running alongside its jogging master or loping along beside a biker. How about dogs gulping fresh air from a pickup truck or an open car window? Gulping and smelling. There's true enthusiasm for the little things of life.

Birds are also wonders of our world. The symmetry of multi-colors blended together on a pheasant's neck, or a pigeon's throat, or a peacock's plumage. The cardinal at our window bird feeder affords meaningful minutes of quiet appreciation for our family. The mother sandpiper and her "broken wing" ploy to entice us to chase her. "Catch me. I'm hurt," she implies as she trots away from her nest of eggs. Geese in their hierarchical *V*'s of flight.

How about bird songs? Orioles, finches, mourning doves, canaries, cardinals. A language of its own. Classical harmonies of their own. Maybe romantic songs. I still love the rural song of the meadow lark which does rhythmically sound like, "Go, wash your feet, you fool." Appreciate them.

Use all of your senses to appreciate life. We take our seeing, hearing, smelling, tasting, and touching for granted at times, don't we? Unfortunately, it's often too late for appreciation after an accident, aging, or disease weakens one of them. Little things that mean a lot. How about the sense of hearing? My life is diminished if I couldn't hear a single beautiful note from a flute, a sigh of love, a sigh of resignation, the ticking of my Grandmother's big wall clock and its quarter-hour chimes, or the reassuring rushing sound of the furnace kicking in on a frigid winter night. And finally, are there any more beautiful sounds than words like, "Mommy," "Daddy," "Auntie," "Grandpa," "Grandma," "Honey," "Darling," "Sweetheart," or your name or mine said meaningfully?

Do you ever listen to silence? Or does silence make you uneasy? Why? Shouldn't silence be peaceful, calm, thoughtful, meditative, and reassuring? Be confident that silence itself is satisfying and nonthreatening, whether in the presence of kings or first dates or just being alone. Listen to the silence. It's beautiful. It's peaceful. It's calming. It's relaxing. The psalmist has a point, "Be still and know that I am God" (Psalm 46:10 NIV). "Silence is golden. Let's get rich."

Edgar Lee Masters has said it all in his poem entitled "Silence," published in an American literature anthology entitled *Songs and Satires*. It presents with dramatic examples a sad and profound truth about human life. It speaks of the silences of the city at night, of love, of rejected love, of illness, of injury, of old age, of death, of failure, of peace of mind, and of the gods. This poem is unquestionably worth finding and reading.

As rewarding as the above may be, it is also satisfying, of course, to listen to "the sounds of music." *Song: a short combination of words and music.* The essay on music earlier in this book focused on lyrics that meet our daily needs. Words or melodies, little ditties or classical overtures, the sounds of our favorite types of music are fulfilling for us all.

Do you ever wonder what that person with the fancy hat in the rear view mirror is singing? Or maybe it's the guy in the pickup beside you at the stoplight. He's obviously singing. What song? How about the pedestrian with the Walkman? She seems to be humming. Appreciate the sounds of music in their various combinations. Maybe even whistling. I like to "whistle while I work" as the Seven Dwarfs did. We do have all kinds of music for mankind, don't we? The sounds of music are endless.

The sounds. Thomas Gray's "Elegy in a Country Churchyard" begins:

> "The curfew tolls the knell of parting day,
> The lowing herd wind slowly o'er the lea,
> The plowman homeward plods his weary way,
> And leaves the world to darkness and to me."

We lived in a small community at one time where the local church's custom was to toll the church bell whenever someone died: 80 times for an 80-year old, 5 times for a 5-year old. All of us would pause in whatever we were doing when that bell was heard. We'd count and reflect. The sounds were profound. It was good.

And don't forget smells. Did you get a whiff of that? Hamburgers and onions frying. Bakery smells. Leaves burning. Sawdust. Freshly mown grass. A freshly bathed and powdered baby. Shampooed hair. Freshly laundered linens. Do appreciate the sense of smell too.

And tastes of cultural cuisines. German brats, French fries, Norwegian lefse, Japanese sushi, Chinese chow mein, English muffins, Italian spaghetti, American burgers, Thai-Korean-Polonaise-Polynesian-Latin-Peruvian-Mexican-African, and so on. Salt. Garlic. Lemon. Champagne. Milk. Be thankful for your taste buds too.

Finally, the little things of touch. How does the pat on the back feel? How about the reassuring hug? How's the hearty handshake? A loving caress? An amorous kiss? Reach out and touch someone. It's a little gesture, but it's so big at the same time! I like you. I appreciate you. It's like a round of applause. I'm attracted to you. I love you. "Touch my hair as you pass my chair, Little Things mean a lot."

All of us can do more than just appreciate however. Give something back to life. Again, we are reminded of the love song that opened this chapter. Love is not little on the yardstick of life's essentials. However, little things help love to grow. At least once a week, praise or communicate with the unsuspecting, deserving, and needy. "Thanks." "Hi." "Thinking of you." "Congrats." "Buck up." Do it in person if you can, but a call or a memo is very good too. Remember the connotations of "You've Got Mail." Go out to praise or comfort people who don't expect to hear from you. *Mark this one on your calendar*, Mondays or Fridays or whenever. Get in the habit of doing such a big "little thing." Will you do it? It's one of the premier principles of positive living.

Love is not little on the yardstick of life's essentials. Little things help love to grow. Love helps little things grow.

Courtesies would seemingly be little things in life. Four-way *STOP* signs are excellent examples of practice in courtesy. Everyone needs to be courteous in turn. Hence, we wait, for three other cars to move on or through. It's good for us. I give thanks for 4-way stops. Courtesy. Open a door for people. Get a chair for someone. Give a sincere smile. Everyone can give "Thanks." Everyone has received. "Thank You. Thank You." "Please" is a kissing cousin of "Thank You." Please your marriage partner. Please by reaching out and "touching" someone at your place of work. It's even more beautiful doing it, then having it done for you.

Here's a final courtesy: a response to courtesy. Do you know how to receive a compliment graciously? It is an art. "Thank you." "That's so kind." I appreciate that a lot." "Wow, that's great, etc." You can do it.

Little things sensed. Little things appreciated. Little things done. Little things can make us or break us. Do things for others. The beauty and the irony is that by doing things for others, we get out of our own skin, forget about ourselves, become part of John Donne's Continent, the world community of man.

The anonymous essay, "I'd Pick More Daisies," might sum up "Little Things":

I'd Pick More Daisies

If I had my life to live over, I'd try to make more mistakes next time. I would relax. I would limber up. I would be sillier than I have been this trip. I know of very few things I would take seriously. I would be crazier. I would be less hygienic. I would take more trips. I would climb more mountains, swim more rivers, and watch more sunsets. I would burn more gasoline. I would eat more ice cream and less beans. I would have more actual troubles and fewer imaginary ones. You see, I am one of those people who lives safely and sensibly and sanely, hour after hour, day after day. Oh, I have had my moments and, if I had it to do over again, I'd have more of them. In fact, I'd try to have nothing else. Just moments, one after another, instead of living so many years ahead of each. I have been one of those people who never goes anywhere without a thermometer, a hot water bottle, a gargle, a raincoat, and a parachute. If I had it to do over again, I would go places and do things and travel lighter that I have.

If I had my life to live over, I would start barefooted in the spring and stay that way later in the fall. I would play hooky more. I wouldn't make such good grades except by accident. I would ride on more merry-go-rounds.

I'd pick more daisies.

Becoming appreciative of the little makes one bigger than one has ever been. The power of addition by subtraction, I believe.

The One-Two Punch For Daily Success

Throughout this book I have recommended two little acts that enrich our daily lives: surprise someone and thank someone. These are little deeds with huge effects.

Surprising someone is more than popping out from a doorway and yelling "boo." It's giving. Give flowers, hugs, compliments, and gifts. Don't be reluctant to creatively surprise. Johann Goethe called gifts "the golden chain by which society is bound together." Write, call, or reward by gift an old teacher, co-worker, teammate, or friend. The possibilities are limitless. But, do it.

Great surprises of my life? A gift picture cube with my wife's picture on top and our four children's pictures on each side. Great surprises I've given or been a part of? A summer surprise 40th birthday on the front lawn for my wife. A surprise gift of fourth row seats to "The Phantom of the Opera" twenty-four hours before show-time. New tires, a grease job, and hail-cracked mirrors unknowingly replaced on a daughter's car while she was out-of-town. Giving is enriching to the soul, regardless of the pocketbook. Use the unexpected regularly. It will invigorate lives.

Thanking someone is the second fundamental for "every day is a good day" satisfaction. Notes are ideal. Have you ever thought of writing a note of thanks to a custodian, a "thank-you" to the mailman, or a note of appreciation to your garbage man. Every person with whom you have contact benefits from a written note of appreciation. It may be a page, a paragraph, or a sentence. Regardless, it will be an invaluable use of your time.

The spoken thanks is more personal than the more tangible written thanks. It's good for immediate gratification. The door was held open for you, a place in line was given to you, a dropped item was secured for you: "Thank You. Thank You." The deserving recipients are all around us. However, the unknowns of our lives, people we encounter out of our home territory, benefit almost as much as those close to us when we take the time to acknowledge them. At the airport, in the plane, in the hotel elevator, at the seafood restaurant, at the ball park, at the concert. "Thank you" is personal. Don't ever be too proud to say it.

Finally, say thanks through your giving. Giving materially and financially. Give both to those who've given to you, and to those who have given nothing to you. Gifts for loved ones, of course, but also say thanks to charitable groups, whether it be the United Fund, the Cancer foundation, the Veteran's clothing drive, the church, or whatever. Say thanks also by giving quality time to your children, your spouse or "significant other," your parents, your employer, and employees. Give of your talents to all of the same.

Thanks can be money, time, or talent. I invest my money in you. I want to serve by giving you my time. I care enough to want to use my talents for our mutual growth and satisfaction. As Catherine Winkworth's hymn so succinctly puts it,

> "Now thank we all our God,
> With heart and hands and voices."

A day that includes a surprise or which gives out thanks through actions or through words of pen or mouth, will always be a worthwhile day.

Executive Holiday, 2005

3M International, the Universe

Dear Manager, Employer, Administrator, CEO, "Boss":

Here are nine tips—nine little things—to show your colleagues and employees that you care. Perhaps also reread the letter to the "Custodial Engineers" from earlier in the book. The tips were learned from a career in the workplace, in the pits, in the arena.

Say "Thanks"...over and over and over. Tell them personally. Tell them publicly. Tell them in writing. Strength is built by praise. This might be the most important premise of the nine. Build up.

Personalize. Strive to treat every one of your employees as an individual. Each has a story. Each has strengths and weaknesses. Get to know them as much as is possible. The more you care about them individually, the stronger your *TEAM* will be: *T*ogether *E*veryone *A*ccomplishes *M*ore.

Keep your door open as much as possible. We want to work for a leader who's accessible and available. Closed doors symbolize barriers, aloofness, and secrecy.

Do not over-theorize. Theories from penthouses are often not the reality of the ground floor. No theory or new philosophy of education will compensate for the lack of communication between pedagogue and learner, between boss and worker. Get to the bottom line, the nuts-and-bolts, the underlying philosophy. Reality over theory. Substance over gloss.

Get into the pits. Spend time in the cubicles, the offices, the rooms, the shops, the factories, the lounges, and the workout rooms.

Substantial, regular time in the pits. Your employees will perform better because you appeared. You'll learn a lot. Reality, not merely theory.

Critique constructively. Build on the strengths by starting with the "good news," then constructively repair or eliminate the weaknesses by turning to the "bad news." Build up; don't tear down.

Listen calmly. Don't jump at rumors. There are two sides to every story. Listen to both. Then combine that with your past experience with the concerned parties and draw your conclusions. Don't presume anything. Judge, but don't be neurotic.

Be loyal. The Beach Boys sing of "being true to your school." Be true to your *Team*. Be true to the people you work with. Go the extra mile with them. Keep their confidences. Stand up and fight for them. Expect the same from them.

Be enthused. Clap, sing, shout. Give a cheer, wave a fist, applaud enthusiastically. It's infectious. We want those types of leaders. Greek: *EN-THEOS: inspired by a god.* That's you, leader.

Sincerely,

Your Employee

*"**B**ut, oh the things I learned from her
When Sorrow walked with me!"*

- Robert Browning Hamilton

CHAPTER TEN

Calm After "The Sky Is Falling" Night!

*S*torms are part of weather patterns as much as sunshine. It is a fact of life. The sky does seemingly fall at times. We don't always experience the fairy tale happy ending. That's reality. We do not always win. That's reality. Cancer, car crashes, divorce, financial failure, poor judgment, circumstantial crises, deaths, betrayals, accidents, wars. That's reality. The Asian proverb goes "All sunshine makes a desert." That's reality.

Abraham Lincoln, en route from losing his job in 1832 to the Presidency in 1860, mingled legislative defeats with victories. He tempered defeats for Speaker, Congressional nomination, Senate appointment, and Vice Presidential nomination with an election to Congress in 1846 and to the Presidency in 1860. Lincoln experienced business failure, rejection for a land office position, death of his sweetheart, and a nervous breakdown in his lifetime. The desert is real in and amongst the sun's rays, wouldn't you say?

Thomas Edison tried 5,000 filaments before he found the answer for our electric light bulb. One win and 4,999 losses? What if he'd have panicked, quit, or given up with the first failure?

Storms do occur. The sky does fall at times. We do end up with the short end of the stick occasionally. What do we do then? We come from a wide range of philosophies: optimistic-pessimistic, religious-atheistic-agnostic, independent-dependent, empathetic-apathetic, philanthropic-penny pinching. All experience the losses and wins, the downs and ups, the valleys and peaks. Oliver Wendell Holmes once said, "Trouble makes us one with every human being in the world." Someone else astutely once observed, "The two toughest things in life are winning and losing." We might disagree with the former, but the point was that winning breeds vanity and conceit. Those who can keep their humility when the world proclaims them as #1 are few and far between. James Grainger in his poem "Solitude" said, "What is fame? An empty bubble; Gold, a transient empty trouble." The axiom is "It's a short distance from the penthouse to the outhouse." What have you done for us lately? Yes, winning can be a challenge too. However, losing assuredly is one of life's "toughest things."

We have been considering the value of living meaningful, peaceful, happy lives throughout this book. Lives that are successful along those lines are, in the language of the world, "winner's" lives. However the reality of life is that if we keep score when you and I play, one of us loses. If six teams run in a cross-country meet, five are losers.

Let's analyze this further. If there are four job openings at this much-respected company, and 201 of us apply, does this mean that 197 of us will be "losers?" One hundred and ninety-seven are "No good?" Or, in another example, if twenty of us want to marry this fantastic, multi-talented, philosophy-compatible, good-looking man or woman, but only one of us gets to: are nineteen of us "out-of-luck," "undesirable" mates or human beings? Let me repeat, if competition is only good for those who finish first, that's not good enough. Why? Because there are many who run the race, many worthwhile competitors.

CALM AFTER "THE SKY IS FALLING" NIGHT! | 151

The popular song "Both Sides Now" by Joni Mitchell said it well: "I've looked at life from both sides now, from win and lose and still somehow, it's life's illusions I recall; I really don't know life at all." It is one of life's illusions that winning is the only thing, that we must win every day, or that losing is fatal. Meg Ryan in the movie, *City of Angels*, plays a heart surgeon who is frustrated when a patient dies on the operating table. "I'm good. I did everything. I did my best. And he still died. I don't understand it." If sports are only good for the winners, then they assuredly are not worthwhile because at least half of the participants lose.

Fundamental principles of living apply to both winning and losing. The winners need to remember that with rare exception their day will come too. They also need to respect those who came out on the short end of the score. Losers need to be gracious to those who prevailed on that particular occasion. At the same time, they should look forward to testing their talents in the next challenge. Life has more in store for both parties.

We have alluded to John Donne's reference to us all, "Every man is a piece of the Continent, a part of the main." Being part of the Continent of man, there will be "The Sky Is Falling" days as well as "Pie in the Sky" days.

This chapter is about dealing with trouble, with losing, and with the "Sky is Falling Night." Losing is reality. How can we deal with it? What can we learn from it? Ella Wheeler Wilcox, in her version of "Solitude," expressed it this way,

> "Laugh, and the world laughs with you;
> Weep, and you weep alone;
> For the sad old earth must borrow its mirth,
> But has trouble enough of its own."

The book of Job in the Old Testament states, "Man is born unto trouble, as the sparks fly upward," (Job 5:7 NIV) and later, "Man that is born of a woman is of few days, and full of trouble. He cometh forth like a flower, and is cut down; he fleeth also as a shadow, and continueth not" (Job 14:1 NIV). Troubles and losing may actually make us want to weep at times. Don't be too proud to do so. Don't be afraid to cry. It's a pure emotion. Let it flow. Sometimes, it will even be of happiness.

The novel *War and Peace* deals with trouble as well as happiness. The alternating sections of the book dealing with wartime and peacetime are symbolic of the valleys and mountaintops of our lives. My wife Mamie has endured a mastectomy for breast cancer, and my daughter has undergone surgery for melanoma, skin cancer, in the past two years. Troubles! Of course. Hurricanes. Earthquakes. Tornadoes. Drought. Floods. Tidal waves. Fame and fortune are inconsequential in comparison to such calamities.

Mother Nature is fearsome. Human nature can be terrifying. Jesus spoke to his disciples about "signs" of these times in Mark 13:7-8 NIV,

When you hear of wars and rumors of wars, do not be alarmed.
Such things must happen, but the end is still to come.
There will be earthquakes in various places and famines.
These are the beginning of birth pains.

"The Sky Is Falling" at times like these. War. Rape. Pillage. Oppression. Prejudice. Discrimination. Ethnic cleansing. The Kosovo-Albania-Serbia-United Nations military conflict with its "cleansing" impetus, the brutal assassinations of over ten thousand Kosovars, and the uprooting of hundreds of thousands of innocent citizens is one gruesome example. The examples of human beings pitted against other human beings of the last half dozen years may well have reminded us of "the End Times."

Terrorism. Human nature has settled on *Terrorism* as the world's watchword since September 11, 2001! Even weekly television shows such as "24," "The Alias," and others capitalize on this theme. It is everyday news today! War and the threat of war. Iraq, Afghanistan, wherever. Bombs, hi-jackings, nuclear warfare, germ warfare, SARS, West Nile disease, Avian Flu, small pox, anthrax, color code alerts for the threats of terrorism! Multiple versions of distress. Worries Incorporated! Armageddon may have been foreshadowed for even the most carefree of us.

Saddam Hussein, Bin Laden, Kim Jong II, and other tyrants and dictators. *Parade* magazine annually lists "The World's 10 Worst Dictators." Consider life under the leaders of Sudan, North Korea, Burma, China, Saudi Arabia, Pakistan, Libya, Turkmenistan, Zimbabwe, and Equatorial Guinea if you don't like your present situation. These are trouble-plagued environments in which one can never win. These examples are more than "birth pains!"

When night is at its darkest, mankind faces the ultimate challenges. Poverty, pollution, pestilence, scarcity, despair. The modern world is extremely challenged economically. World hunger in Afghanistan, Uganda, Nigeria, Pakistan, or Cambodia. Financial crises from weather-related calamities such as hurricanes, floods, tidal waves, and earthquakes. The Gulf Coast devastation of Hurricane Katrina is a prime example. Estimates are that damages will exceed $200 billion. Fiscal responsibility, whether it is personal or national debt doesn't matter. Our resources are not endless! We live in a world of challenges!

Our world is facing off politically through varied dictatorial, communist, and democratic systems of government: Iraq, North Korea, China, and the United States being cases in point. Internationally, our world citizenship is being challenged philosophically by rebels and insurgents opposing Western involvement in Middle Eastern government, for example, the struggles in Iraq and Afghanistan. Even the "little" wars like those being waged therein leave indelible scars. Over 2000 American soldiers (and counting) have given their lives in the Middle East, to say nothing of the loss of innocent civilians' lives on both sides. Financially too: $300 billion has been spent on the above-mentioned two "little" wars. In those two areas of conflict alone, expenditures are approximated to be $855 billion in another decade.

"The Sky Is Falling" world is here. Luke in his New Testament gospel says, "From everyone who has been given much, much will be demanded; and from the one who has been entrusted with much, much more will be asked" (Luke 12:48 NIV). Guess who has been "given much," America? We are citizens of a world wrestling economically with "the Haves and the Have-Nots" strata. We of the Western world keep habitually playing our twin national anthems of greed, "I Want What I Want When I Want It!" and "All I Want Is All There Is and Then Some." Can we in any way be worse stewards of our blessings than by, quite frankly, hoarding them?

Finally, we are citizens of a world threatened morally by every vice and temptation conceivable to man's intellect. Have total freedom, "Everything Goes" attitudes, and free love amorality ever led to anything other than crumbling civilizations? Pride, arrogance, selfishness, and moral deterioration did bring down the great Roman and Greek civilizations several thousand years ago. We're walking in some of those same misguided footsteps today. We have abused our privileges and freedoms more and more over the course of time. Decaying from self-indulgence within and exhibiting little moral backbone without, just like those ancient cultures, what have we become?

Troubles. Emergencies. Storms. Losses. Challenges. All these "Glass is half empty" examples seem to be part of our daily lives. They might call into question our 21st century "progress" and "advances." Is the sky falling? Is it the "End"? Have we had enough?

Grace Noll Crowell has a poetic response:

To One in Sorrow

Let me come in where you are weeping, friend,
And let me take your hand.
I, who have known a sorrow such as yours,
Can understand
Let me come in…I would be very still
Beside you in your grief,
I would not bid you cease your weeping, friend,
Tears bring relief.
Let me come in…I would only breathe a prayer,
And hold your hand,
For I have known a sorrow such as yours
And understand.

There Will Be Day. There Will Be Night. What Shall We Do When The Sun Goes Down? How Can We Find Calm After The "Sky Is Falling" Night?

James Morrison's *Masterpieces of Religious Verse* includes the following succinct, poignant poem by Robert Browning Hamilton:

Pleasure and Sorrow

I walked a mile with Pleasure,
She chattered all the way,
But left me none the wiser
For all she had to say.

I walked a mile with Sorrow,
And ne'er a word said she;
But, oh, the things I learned from her
When Sorrow walked with me!

As mentioned earlier in the book, we as a family walked a mile with sorrow in the spring of 1998 as our thirty-four year old son suffered a brain aneurysm while running. Twenty-one hospital days, three in a comatose stage, were a Black Hole of despair. "Oh, the things *we* learned when Sorrow walked with us that March!" I know I had never debated my Maker before. I amazed myself at how unabashedly emotionally I dared to dialogue with Him. I also know I've never been so thankful in my life as when Kyle came out of it. He returned to work less than half a year later with only minor residual effects.

All, thankfully, continues to be well today—two daughters, a heavier work load, and seven years later. Every member of our family appreciates a raindrop, a sunset, a flower bud, a job, an herb, a hamburger, a cool glass, a warm cup, a perfume, a smell of burning leaves, a hug, a kiss, a song, a church bell more than ever before because of this near-tragedy. "Oh, the things we learned from Sorrow." We learned that, indeed, we are of few days. Seize the moments. Appreciate them. That is a start to becoming.

What if trouble strikes me? What if I lose? What if I come to dying and I haven't lived? What if I'm "successful," and yet life still lacks meaning? What if I have my life before me, but I sense no direction therein? What if I've loved and lost? What if money eludes me, deludes me, or betrays me? What if I'm ill-fated health-wise? What if "The Sky Falls"? Hamlet said it,

"To be or not to be, that is the question.
Whether 'tis nobler in the mind to suffer
The slings and arrows of outrageous fortune,
Or to take arms against a sea of trouble,
And, by opposing, end them."

Harold B. Walker composed a pocket essay to possibly help us:

You can think about your problems or you can worry about them, and there is a vast difference between the two. Worry is thinking that has turned toxic. It is jarring music that goes round and round and never comes to either climax or conclusion. Thinking works its way through problems to conclusions and decisions; worry leaves you in a state of tensely suspended animation. When you worry, you go over the same ground endlessly and come out the same place you started. Thinking makes progress from one place to another; worry remains static. The problem of life is to change worry into thinking and anxiety into creative action.

You've maybe heard the mathematics of "Why Worry?"

- 40% will never happen, for anxiety is the result of a tired mind.
- 30% concerns old decisions which cannot be altered.
- 12% centers in criticism, mostly untrue, made by people who feel inferior.
- 10% is related to my health that worsens while I worry, and only
- 8% is "legitimate," showing that life does have real problems that may be met head-on when I have eliminated senseless worries.

Try such "thinking" and some of the above mathematics!

In the old *McGuffey's Reader*, is a story about the clock that had been running for a long, long time on the mantelpiece. One day the clock began to think about how many times during the year ahead it would have to tick. It counted up the seconds...31,536,000 in the year...and the old clock just got too tired and said, "I can't do it," and stopped right there. When somebody reminded the clock that it did not have to tick the 31,536,000 seconds all at one time, but rather one by one, it began to run again and everything was all right (*Treasure Chest*, Nenien C. McPherson, Jr.). I unquestionably believe it's mind over matter in the majority of life's situations. It's thinking over worrying.

For many years, I had a laminated note card taped to the bottom of my middle desk drawer. I would see its four words every time I opened the drawer. The words were "This Too Shall Pass." If I was feeling like King of the World, or if I was feeling like the worst of the world, "This Too Shall Pass." Paraphrased: there will be wins; there will be losses. You'll be good; you'll be not so good. There will be war; there will be peace. It's a humbling truism. Grandma Moses, in *My Life's History*, illustrated it this way, "Then Anna was born, so I had four babies to care for. But we got along very nice till the children got the scarlet fever, that was a hard year, but it passed on like all the rest." This too shall pass, whatever the circumstances.

Hardships, tough times, calamities, and tragedies make us or break us, depending on our toughness. That toughness is developed under fire. Life's catastrophic forest fires, as well as the nuisance brush fires, all test our mettle. We need a philosophy of life that undergirds all that we embody, say, and do. Our philosophy must reassure us that storms pass and we are strong.

Eli Wiesel's Jews in Nazi WWII prison camps of the novel *Night* had their beliefs tested far beyond what most of us will ever experience. The damnation of this diabolical epoch of human history cannot be lost on even the most insensitive among us. This is not to say that you may not have suffered your own hellish stresses and crises of life. You've probably had your personal convictions examined too if moral and ethical questions have been thrown at you.

Some trees seem to bend with each windstorm. Others snap and break. Some seem imperturbable. John F. Kennedy said, "Only in winter can you tell which trees are truly green. Only when the winds of adversity blow can you tell whether an individual or a country has courage and steadfastness." Are you a weeping willow or a mighty oak?

All of us are going to feel like the "Sky Is Falling" at some time. We are probably going to get "bent out of shape" over some things. We may stumble and even fall. The mark of a man or a woman is not that one falls, but rather what one does after one falls. Harvard has a legend about the late Le Baron Russell Briggs, a longtime beloved dean, who once asked a student why he had failed to complete an assignment. "I wasn't feeling very well, Sir," said the student. "Mr. Smith," said the Dean, "I think that in time you may perhaps find that most of the work of the world is done by people who aren't feeling very well."

Have you ever felt scarred by life and its experiences? Like one of Sherwood Anderson's "gnarled apples" from his book *Winesburg, Ohio*? Not a plump, shining apple, but rather a "gnarled apple." If you have ever felt "gnarled," you have sensed "The Sky is Falling Night" phenomenon. Consider, then, Anderson's metaphor of life.

"The apples have been taken from the trees by the pickers. On the trees are left only a few gnarled apples that the pickers have rejected. One nibbles at them, and they are delicious. Into a little round place at the side of the apple has been gathered all its sweetness. Only a few know the sweetness of the twisted apples."

Symbolically, every life has incomparable sweetness. Cherish the sweetness in yourself.

We as humans all unquestionably have our moments of feeling "gnarled." At times, that might actually be illness or physical scars or maladies, but more frequently, the "ailments" are procrastination, indecisiveness, frustration, or laziness. At these times, we must "press on." Afraid? Risky?

> "It's a risk to have a husband, a risk to have a son;
> A risk to pour your confidence out to anyone;
> A risk to pick a daisy, for there's sure to be a cop,
> A risk to go on living, but a greater risk to stop."
>
> (Ruth Mason Rice)

It's so tough though?

> "Dr. Cane, finding a flower under the Humboldt glacier, was more affected by it because it grew beneath the lip and cold bosom of the ice, than he would have been by the most gorgeous blooming garden. So some single struggling grace in the heart of one far removed from Divine influences may be dearer to God than a whole catalog of virtues in the life of one more favored of Heaven. As in nature, as in art, so in grace; it is rough treatment that gives souls, as well as stones, their luster. The more the diamond is cut, the brighter it sparkles; and in what seems hard dealing, there God has no end in view but to perfect His people."
>
> (Kenneth Sylvan Guthrie)

The Bible speaks to life's ups and downs in Romans 5:3-5 NIV: "But we also rejoice in our sufferings, because we know that suffering produces perseverance; perseverance, character; and character, hope." Ralph Waldo Emerson philosophized, "When it is dark enough, men see the stars." After the darkness, the dawn. You can't see a rainbow without the rain. Hoping and dreaming are the sun's rays through the raindrops which makes rainbows.

An internationally renowned surgeon once said, "A man can live three weeks without food, three days without water, and three minutes without air, but he cannot live three seconds without hope." This doctor was speaking to a group of mothers of amputee children who were attending a free clinic. Despair was written on the face of everyone in the audience, for each child in the room was in the sad plight of having a limb missing. "Have hope and love," the doctor advised the parents. "That combination, under God, is unconquerable. Enlisting the rich resources of modern medicine, it is highly possible that you will see your child lead a normal life and play his role in society when he is grown." (Reuben K.Youngdahl, *Living God's Way*). Martin Luther King's classic quote of hope epitomizes this need for all of mankind: "I have a dream."

In the Appendix of characters for *The Sound and the Fury*, there's an awesome epitaph to Dilsey, the stalwart Negro mammy of William Faulkner's classic novel. The finale belongs to Dilsey, just as the final chapter of the book is hers. Only two words are used to characterize her: "They endured." The Dilseys of the world endure; they persevere. Dilsey suffers and endures. Read about her. She's the flower in the glacier.

Life unquestionably has peaks and valleys, sunny radiant skies and stormy "Falling Skies." Whatever you do, compete. A poet says it all.

Don't Quit

When things go wrong, as they sometimes will,
When the road you're trudging seems all uphill,
When the funds are low and the debts are high,
And you want to smile, but you have to sigh,
When care is pressing you down a bit,
Rest, if you must, but don't you quit.
Life is queer with its twists and turns
As every one of us sometimes learns.

And many a failure turns about,
When he might have won had he stuck it out.
Don't give up though the pace seems slow
You may succeed with another blow.

Success is failure turned inside out,
The silver tint of the clouds of doubt.
And you never can tell how close you are,
It may be near when it seems so far,
So stick to the fight when you're hardest hit,
It's when things seem worse
That you must not quit.

(Author Unknown)

Harry Emerson Fosdick put it this way,

"Most of us can afford to take a lesson from the oyster. The most extraordinary thing about the oyster is this. Irritations get into his shell. He does not like them; he tried to get rid of them. But when he cannot get rid of them, he settles down to make of them one of the most beautiful things in the world. He uses the irritation to do the loveliest thing that an oyster ever has a chance to do. If there are irritations in our lives today, there is only one prescription: make a pearl. It may have to be a pearl of patience, but, anyhow, make a pearl. And it takes faith and love to do it."

Listen to these additional affirmations. Paul Simon's song lyrics, "Like a bridge over troubled water, I will lay me down," speak to closure of these realities of life's down times. The medieval knights had a similar rallying creed: "I am wounded, but I am not slain. I will lay me down to rest, and on the morrow I shall rise to fight again." Psalm 46:1 NIV encourages us with, "God is our hope and strength: a very present help in trouble." The 10th Rung "Song for the Evening" recommended earlier in this book affirms us,

> "Sun of my soul, Thou Savior dear,
> It is not night if Thou be near:
> Oh, may no earthborn cloud arise
> To hide Thee from Thy servant's eyes!"

Another song, this time by George Asof, emphasizes the positive in this way, "What's the use of worrying? It was never worthwhile, so, *Pack Up Your Troubles* in your old kit bag and smile, smile, smile."

Lay me down. Keep the faith. Pack up our troubles. Believe. Smile. If we will heed these suggestions, our strength will be renewed. An unknown author penned these lines, "When faced with a mountain, I will not quit. I will keep on striving until I climb over, find a pass through, tunnel underneath, or simply stay and turn the mountain into a gold mine, with God's help."

You may have read Rudyard Kipling's famous poem "If." Though it's a paraphrase, do you remember lines like, "If you can keep your head...wait...dream; If you can bear to hear the truth twisted...face triumph and disaster...hold on...talk with crowds...walk with kings...give sixty seconds worth of distance run...you'll be a Man, my son!"?

Those qualities should help us immensely "If" we can add them to our lives. What is more, "You'll be a woman or man, my daughter or son." Surviving the blast furnace of life does result in tempered steel. Becoming tempered steel is to become as strong as man can become. The sky may be falling, but "This Too Shall Pass."

There Shall Be No More Death!

*"He will wipe away every tear from their eyes. There will
be no more death or mourning or crying or pain, for the old
order of things has passed away.*

*He who was seated on the throne said, I am making
everything new!"*

(Revelation 21:4-5 NIV)

Death! One of my first encounters with death was when I was six
years old. I was skipping stones among the lily pads in an old country
side ditch that was always filled with water. I was enjoying the two to
three dozen frogs who would jump into the water every time a stone
splashed by. Then dramatically the morning changed. One of my
throws hit one of the bigger frogs. He flipped, yellow belly up. He
floated. He was dead. The fun was over.

When I was nine years old, my buddy Raymond and I were hunting pheasants one fine October day. October 12th to be exact. Not
having any real luck, we decided to explore the abandoned buildings
on the old Jelle farm. Coming out of the ram shackled house, we
stared down an incline into the undergrowth of a small grove. "Look,
Paul, someone hung a dummy down there." The eeriness of the
comment was justified. Two nine-year-olds, after a cautious circling
into the woods, had eyes opened, noses repulsed, and souls shaken by
human death and decomposition. Three weeks earlier a man had taken
his life in this deserted backwoods area. Since then, October 12th has
never been strictly Columbus Day.

I have never really liked to think of death. I didn't like it when at
14, my dog Buster of the same age, died. I had tears in my eyes when
the video "Brian's Song," a tribute to the Chicago Bears' Brian Piccolo's

courageous fight against cancer, concluded. I vividly remember where I was standing when the announcement was made over the P.A. system of the high school which I was teaching at that President J.F.K. had been assassinated. The accidental death of Princess Diana in recent years was another reminder of the abruptness with which life can end. Attending the funeral of a 19-year-old former basketball player who nine months earlier had won All-Conference honors was not a good day in my life. And then, of course, we have had the senseless decimation of 168 lives in the Oklahoma City bombing, the unexplainable high school massacre of 14 people in Littleton, Colorado, 40 plus lives taken in a 250 mph tornado in Oklahoma, the murder of seven young people at a Baptist church songfest in Fort Worth, Texas, the September 11, 2001 deaths of 3,025 people in the World Trade Center crashes, 372 Belarus deaths of school children and adults, 230,000 plus in the 2004 Far Eastern tidal waves, and more than 50 killed and more than 700 injured in London's terrorist attack. Abd-El-Kader's "black camel, which kneels at the gates of all," shuffles on through the dust of time.

I've been thinking more of death as I've gotten older. Anyone's funeral should remind all of us to *NOT* avoid thinking about it. My ever reliable Oxford *Dictionary of Quotations* has 270 entries under "death." Emily Dickinson reminds us in her poem, "Because I could not stop for Death...He kindly stopped for me...The Carriage held but just Ourselves...And Immortality." Alan Seeger put it this way, "I have a rendezvous with Death, at some disputed barricade." Shakespeare, in *Richard II* (Act III, Sc. 2, L. 61), says, "The worst is death, and death will have his day."

In 1989 Mike and the Mechanics popularized the song "The Living Years." It has a strong message for every one of us in regards to preparing for death. The theme is expressed herein: "I just wish I could have told him in the living years." The refrain haunts us through the chorus: "Say it loud, say it clear. You can listen as well as you hear. It's too late when we die to admit we don't see eye-to-eye." Listen and become more thoughtful if it applies.

Earlier in this book, I mentioned not being prepared for the long distance telephone call in 1962 which informed me that my father had had a heart attack and had died. "Wait...I need to tell him a couple things...like how much I *really* love him." I wasn't there that morning when my father passed away. I should have told him more during his years with us. Let's all remember to say the things that should be said now, during "The Living Years."

We're never ready, but we do need to prepare ourselves for death. It's reality: the death of a pet dog or cat, or even a favorite flowering crab tree, to say nothing of a colleague, a family member, or ourselves. I mentioned earlier in this book once living in a small community which followed the old European custom of tolling the church bell whenever anyone died. They'd toll the number of years of that person's life. It could be 2, 24, or 92. Community life would stop when the tolling began. It was good for us. John Donne was right, "And therefore, never send to know for whom the bell tolls." It was a type of preparedness.

Does death frighten some of us? Probably. Hamlet said it was "The dread of something after death, the undiscovered country from whose bourn no traveler returns, puzzles the will." Is there more? Is it good or bad? Hamlet's "To be or not to be" is really, "to live or to die." His soliloquy goes on, "To die, to sleep; to sleep: per chance to dream: ay, there's the rub; For in that sleep of death what dreams may come when we have shuffled off this mortal coil, must give us pause." (*Hamlet*, Act 3, Sc. 1).

I want to be unafraid. I want to say with John Gunther, who wrote of his teenage son's death, in the book, *Death Be Not Proud*: "Be not proud, though some have called thee mighty and dreadful, for thou art not so." I want to be unafraid with the apostle Paul in I Corinthians 15:55 NIV of the New Testament, "Where, O death, is thy victory? Where, O death, is thy sting?" Read the contemporary, non-fiction best seller *Tuesdays with Morrie* for a great courageous story of a man facing death.

The best advice I could offer any of us in preparation for death is ironically borrowed from Meyer Wolfsheim in F. Scott Fitzgerald's *The Great Gatsby*. I've used the example earlier in this book, but it bears repeating. He's Gatsby's buddy, but he doesn't come to Gatsby's funeral. "Let us learn to show our friendship for a man when he's alive and not after he's dead. After that, my own rule is to let everything alone."

I heard recently of a man in his 80's who "celebrated" his own wake at a banquet. He said, "I'm about 'there.' Wouldn't it better if while alive, the person got to hear all those nice things said about him at a funeral?" He has a point. The following verse also echoes these thoughts:

> "If you think that praise is due him.
> Now's the time to slip it to him,
> For he cannot read his tombstone
> When he's dead."

"Of all sad things 'mong mice and men, the saddest was it might have been." Open your mouth before "the bell tolls."

If death and taxes are inevitable, how can I be ready? There's only one way. I need a solid belief system. Mine is simple. There is "a far, far better place I go to" as Sydney Carton asserts at the end of Charles Dickens' *Tale of Two Cities*. I also love the words from John F. Kennedy's funeral anthem, "My hope is built on nothing less, than Jesus' blood and righteousness." And the chorus, "On Christ, the solid rock, I stand; All other ground is sinking sand." Paul, in his New Testament letter to the Romans says, "For I am persuaded that neither death, nor life, nor angels, nor principalities, nor powers, nor things present, nor things to come, nor height, nor depth, nor any other creature, shall be able to separate us from the love of God, which is in Christ Jesus, our Lord" (Romans 8:38 NIV).

Having a belief system allows one to plant one's feet, to brace for the hurricanes of life such as death, and yet to be comfortable in the knowledge that your head will still be "up high" after the storm.

"He will wipe every tear from their eyes. *There will be no more death* or mourning or crying or pain, for the old order of things has passed away. He who was seated on the throne said, 'I am making everything new!'"

(Revelation 21:4-5 NIV)

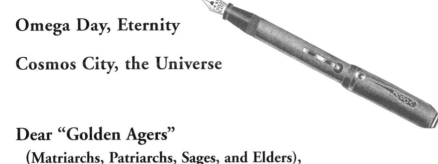

Omega Day, Eternity

Cosmos City, the Universe

Dear "Golden Agers"
(Matriarchs, Patriarchs, Sages, and Elders),

"It takes about ten years to get used to how old you are."

(Unknown)

"Age doesn't matter unless you're a cheese."

(Billie Burke)

Youth, middle-aged, elderly, what more can we ask than "to be remembered?" Remembered, respected, utilized, loved. If you've made it to the "Golden Years," "The Twilight Time," the "Winter of our Discontent," you've accomplished a lot, haven't you? You've seen, done, and experienced almost everything. Yes, you want to have left footprints. Yes, you want respect and love. You've been our age too! Listen to what was learned. It makes your lives useful. We all will covet those things for our last days.

This letter is long overdue. It is simply a "Thank You" letter. You are appreciated. Probably more than we have told you. You are loved. That is the most important thing. Thank you for your lives and efforts. Thank you. For all you've done. For all you've been. For all you are. Matriarchs, Patriarchs, Sages, and Elders: we thank you all.

Honor our dignity, you say. Well, I guess. You've earned your spurs. We need to dignify your venerable years. Your contributions to our lives and to society itself deserve honor. You deserve our heart-felt appreciation in your "Twilight Time." Your feelings should be proud ones. Those feelings deserve our respect. You should be proud too.

Whitey Aus coined this P.R.I.D.E. acronym and shared it with colleagues. I salute your Golden Age dignity and pride with a minor paraphrase of it.

> *P* is for the power you generated.
> *R* is for the unique role you fulfilled.
> *I* is for the inspiration you gave.
> *D* is for your determination.
> *E* is for your enthusiasm. Thanks!

Useful. I want to be useful. Even when retired, I believe you want to be useful. The contemporary novel and movie, *The Horse Whisperer*, by Nicholas Evans, has this insightful excerpt: "Do you fear anything, Tom Booker?" "Yes," Tom replies, "I'm afraid of growing old and of not being useful." How about you? I think most people want to be useful throughout their lives. Fight the good fight all the way. "Die with your spurs on." Whatever. The next paragraph is a surefire way to being useful and being able to "smile the rest of your days," as the song goes.

Share. Sharing is useful. Who has more to share than the person who has had many years of experience? A diary, a journal, a photo album, a home movie, a videotape of past experiences: all are excellent to share. One step better is to speak to the "Source." Someone who lived through the Depression, who participated in a war, who has dealt with the agonies and ecstasies of daily life. Pick the brains of the sages. You may have to initiate the conversation. I'll never forget the retired 80-plus-year-old banker, Mr. Frank Gerry, of St. Charles, Minnesota. My wife and I rented his upstairs for three years in an early career teaching-coaching assignment. If you "asked" this distinguished Freemason about almost anything, he was "off and running," and you'd have a diplomatic challenge to get away in less than an hour. I'm sure he preferred two plus hours at any sitting. You know what? It made his day to have a chance to share. We'd better utilize such sources. Initiate the conversation. If we don't, we both lose. Sharing makes a day worthwhile. It makes one feel useful.

Loved. Pups need it. Babies need it. Gardens, lawns, and ball fields thrive on it. Young children are nourished by it. Cars, windows, teens, and newlyweds shine from it. Cats, horses and cows, parents and mid-lifers percolate when it is received. The giver of love grows from giving it. It's an absolute. Of course, grandparents want to give silver dollars or the like. The seniors, Methuselahs, the centarians-octogenarians-sexagenarians want, need, and will thrive, or wither, on love, or the lack of it. Robert Browning in one of his poems, "Rabbi Ben Ezra," speaks of "Grow old along with me! The best is yet to be." That's love. It's the Life Force.

Exercise. Be active, but be careful. It's great to hear of those entering into "the sear, the yellow leaf of life," as Macbeth calls it, who are working out at fitness clubs, who are playing in 60+ and 70+ slow pitch softball leagues, who are playing golf and tennis, and, at the minimum, are walking. We walked before we ran. It's O.K. to return to that. "Activity" would also apply to being a participant in life. If concerts, dramas, museums, and art galleries were good for you at twenty and forty, why not also now? The mind, body, and spirit are stimulated and enriched by exercise and active participation in life.

Conversely, inactivity atrophies all that you are. Consider the prisoner returning from solitary confinement. Body, mind, speech are all stunted. Stay active. The "Be careful" admonition is simply this: it's permissible to go more slowly. Be smart. Be active without being stressful. Walking over jogging spares knee joints. Analogous mental exertions are easy to come by. A Roger Winston concert may be a better choice than The Rolling Stones, for instance. Be active intelligently...a version of "Hasten Slowly."

Learning. Solon, one of Greece's Seven Sages, added this characteristic to desirable living for the elderly. "I grow old ever learning many things." I know continuing to learn in one's senior years will keep the mind young, just as being physically active keeps the body young. "If you don't use it, you'll lose it." Keep doing crossword puzzles. Keep reading. Keep listening. Keep inquiring. I go to Barnes & Noble

Bookstore and I witness, "So much to learn, so little time." No intake: no output. Without physical and mental activity, we are guaranteed apathy, stagnation, or death on the vine. Curiosity will not kill the wise old cat; curiosity will keep the old cat wise. I do shake my head at times over the irony of finally becoming relatively wise through age, study, and experience, only to enter Shakespeare's Seventh Age of Man, "Sans teeth, sans eyes, sans taste, sans everything." I wish when we knew the most, we could use the most. Read the entire soliloquy by Jacques in *As You Like It.* You probably have heard its introduction, "All the world's a stage and all the men and women merely players...and one man in his time plays many parts, his acts being 'Seven Ages'." You'll smile, laugh, and cry at the validity of the description of the various stages from infancy to senility.

Finally, Have No Fear. Contemporary society is trying to capitalize on this slogan. Pick-up trucks, T-shirts, team mottoes, a fighting philosophy, etc. Listen to Mahatma Gandhi, "Each night when I go to sleep, I die. And the next morning, when I awake, I am reborn." Have no fear. Live each day to the fullest. Respect all; fear nothing. It has its merits. Dylan Thomas: "Do Not Go Gentle Into That Good Night." Solon again, "Call no man happy before he dies; he is at best but fortunate." No Fear.

Well, if you can incorporate most of these principles into the autumns and winters of your lives, you should have what Macbeth in his last season coveted, "that which should accompany old age, As honor, love, obedience, and troops of friends." May it be yours. Thank you, veterans. Thank you, wise ones. Thank you. You are loved and appreciated.

Sincerely,

The "Other" Generations

P.S. The Elysian Fields will be blessed when you arrive.

"*I made the joyous discovery that ten minutes of belly laughter is worth two hours of anesthesia.*"

- Norman Cousins

CHAPTER ELEVEN

Having Fun, Fun, Fun While Becoming!

*I*t was the suburban conference championship baseball game. The score was 1-1. Jogging from our visitors' dugout to my 3rd base coaching box, I was wearing my stern, concerned, competitive game-face. As I passed home plate, the voice of veteran umpire Gary Rover broke my concentration, "Are you having fun, Coach?" It was perfect. It was such a valid question. My answer would have been so indicting if I were honest. We need to enjoy the moments, not stress out over them. We all need to find pleasure in the things we are doing. As Cole Porter put it in his song "Just One of Those Things,"

> "So goodbye dear, and Amen,
> Here's hoping we meet now and then,
> It was great fun
> But it was just one of those things."

In this closing chapter, let's consider bringing fun, enjoyment, pleasure, and amusement to even the most "simple things" in our daily lives. Fun is part of life's fulfillment too. Fun, enjoyment, pleasure, amusement. Let's identify them in six areas of our existence.

Family: it was fun for this father seeing several of his children being born in hospital delivery rooms. So much fun that I still can feel those tears of happiness oozing out of the corners of my eyes.

Work: farming, coaching and teaching were mine. Showing champion Aberdeen Angus cattle at the State Fair was fun. Winning athletically was fun too, en route to and in various State Tournaments and even a twenty-one game winning streak. Having a student win a little money and get her creative composition published in a national writing contest was fun.

Companionship, courtship, and marriage: it was fun when Mamie said "Yes" to my proposal of marriage. It's fun forty-seven years later to know that she's even more wonderful now than she was then.

Daily food, clothing, and shelter: it's fun to have orange juice and a heaping bowl of cereal topped with fresh strawberries. It's fun to have both rainwear and swimwear in the closets. It's enjoyable to have a well-functioning thermostat for air-conditioning in the summer as well as for our gas furnace in Minnesota sub-zero winters.

Hobbies and free time: it is fun walking Trail Ridge in Estes Park of the Rocky Mountain chain. It is fun walking in the Pacific Ocean off San Diego Bay. It is fun surveying the Atlantic Ocean off Cape Cod.

Service: it is fun having the best scholars in one's college prep classroom be thankful at year's end for the academic labors that we endure. It is fun having renegade athletes shape up their lives and lifestyles in order to earn a starting position and All-Conference honors on a team.

FUN. Why not a chapter on finding fun in our everyday existence? Assess your daily routines. Am I having fun or not? Does my day include opportunities to smile? Even the "great ones" look better with smiles on their faces. Consider the perpetual stoic, San Antonio's Tim

Duncan, the most valuable player of the NBA. He radiated again in 2005 when his Spurs once more clinched a world title. Even he can smile!

How about "The Rock," Brianna Scurry, the soccer goalie for the women's World Cup soccer champions from the United States? I'd call it refreshing a couple years ago to see the impassive faced Scurry break out into awesome smiles of jubilation after her team emerged victorious from the tension-filled penalty kick shoot-out following 120 scoreless minutes. Apparent stoicism can be a valuable asset for a focused competitor during a contest. However, it's beautiful to see the real person who drops the "game face" once it's over in exchange for a smile, and maybe even charismatic charm and magnetism. Warm someone's heart today with a smile. Smiles and fun are good health for all of us. Endorphins.

Let's laugh. Endorphin load! It has been proven healthful. I'll never forget the experience of Norman Cousins, editor of the *Saturday Review* magazine. In 1960 he was diagnosed with symptoms of a debilitating spinal disease and cancer. "There I made the joyous discovery that ten minutes of belly laughter is worth two hours of anesthesia." He said he went on a marathon of humor: books, movies, comedy of every sort. The symptoms disappeared. He wrote a book about the experience called *Anatomy of an Illness.* Endorphins do neutralize worries and revitalize lives. Make laughter part of your daily vitamins.

Family

Oh, my! We all need the closeness, the support, the love of family. We all need the fun of family picnics, holidays, birthdays, reunions, and anniversaries. We don't all have this solid base of operations. I implore those of you without any real feeling of "family," those of you from broken homes, or no real "home" environment at all, to still study "families" and to carefully note what you're missing. As a result, make an eternal vow that your children will not experience the same emptiness...and lack of fun. Vow that there will be enjoyment, love, and support for those closest to you. I've seen people do it. Some of those families are stronger than normal because they know what they've been missing. They don't "take it for granted." They appreciate and cultivate togetherness better because of having suffered. Either way, make family as much fun as you can.

One of America's finest families had four daughters excel in the classroom and on the volleyball-basketball courts of Apple Valley High School, Apple Valley, Minnesota, from 1987 through 1996. Record-setters locally, and recruited nationally, all four "were excellent students and athletes with tremendous values. They never had a prima-donna attitude and were as humble as the kid struggling to do just one thing right in his or her life. They are model citizens. It doesn't happen by accident. Harold and Barb Shudlick, their parents, deserve tremendous credit," shared Walt Weaver, their volleyball coach.

The parents' credo, regardless of athletics, Science Fair, or music, was basically: "**Have fun**. Try hard. Do your best. Be there to guide and be positive. We never tried to say, 'You played lousy' nor 'you played great.' We tried to ask, 'Did you have fun?'"

> For one moment, a couple summers ago, the Shudlick sisters were together again, back from college, sharing a basketball. "There was basketball at open gym and all four of us got on the same team," said Susan, the youngest. "As kids we played together for a long time, but it usually was 2-on-2. I don't think all four of us had played together before. It was a lot of fun!"
>
> (*Minneapolis Tribune*, "Sports," October 18, 1995)

A lesson for all of us here, when speaking with youthful participants after any activity, please initially ask only, "Did you have fun?" That's the bottom line, not whether they won or lost. This is critical to their having a healthy enjoyment of life.

Work and Fun

Families must work together and play together. How about raking and bagging leaves as well as baiting fish hooks and catching fish together? Working on the house together—painting, adding to the patio, garage cleaning, resurfacing the driveway—all are good family bonding opportunities. I think you'll find they are natural springboards to socializing together (a play, a concert), participating together (softball, picnicking), vacationing together (a resort weekend or a week out-of-state), and worshiping together (church, synagogue, religious activities).

How does it go, "A family that sweats together gets together"? Or was it, "plays and prays together, stays together"? Or was it, "learns to run together, has fun together"? Maybe the poet Ogden Nash had a point in his verse entitled "Family Court":

> "One would be in less danger
> From the wiles of the stranger
> If one's own kin and kith
> Were more fun to be with."

Jimmy Buffet, a contemporary composer-entertainer-musician, was being interviewed on network television recently and he emphatically marveled at how, "I just love my work." Now, obviously, most of us have "dog" days interspersed with our good days even if we love our jobs, but how gratifying it is to enjoy our workplace. That enjoyment may be from the challenge, the satisfaction, the compensation of the work itself, a combination of the above, or it may stem from the co-workers and the environment in which one works.

The architect, Alquist in *R.U.R.* was right, "There was virtue in toil and weariness." If you haven't found pleasure in tired, sweaty muscles being soothed in a warm bath or a hot shower, you need to add this experience to your days. Gus Kahn and Raymond Egan composed the song, "Ain't We Got Fun?" Work doesn't seem quite so laborious if we can have fun.

Fun in Courtship, Love, Marriage, and Sex

Yes! Now courtship might be the most threatening because of the newness of the acquaintanceship. However, from the first date on, one would like to be known as "Fun to be with," rather than "No fun," right? I'm not sure if Dorothy Sayers was a football fan or not, but her quote aptly applies to fun in our love lives. "I admit it's better to punt than to be punted, and a desire to have all the fun is nine-tenths of the law of chivalry." Be fun to be with, before and after marriage. Be funny if you can. Drop your mask, your inhibitions. Be as spontaneous as you can. Lighten up. "Smile awhile and give your face a rest."

Fun in human and animal sexuality has been noted to inherently include nudging, tickling, poking, as well as touching, caressing, and fondling. Fun can be the presence, the proximity, of your partner. Fun can be a smile across a room and the anticipation of that distance being bridged. Would it be fun enjoying an exceptional meal together? Would it be fun enjoying favorite snacks together? Is it more fun sitting on a hillside or on a mountainside? Is it more fun to be by a lakeside, at a river's edge, or on an ocean front, watching the sunset? Is it more fun anticipating having children together, or having children together?

The Lord God of *Genesis* 2:18 NIV was right, "It is not good for man to be alone. I will make a helpmate for him." Fun together could be jokes, the amusement park, the fun house or a comic drama, but there is even more. Have fun courting, loving, marrying each other... and sexuality will be intrinsic to all of them. As Woody Allen in his 1977 film *Annie Hall* said candidly, "Sex was the most fun I ever had without laughing."

Sex is a serious, beautiful experience. It is a gift but not a toy. Sex is the ultimate expression of love, but sex is not the oxymoron, free love. It should be reserved for people totally dedicated to each other. Its purpose, significance, and meaningfulness should be honored. Yes, cynics, I hear you! However, this book has been trying to spotlight for you a meaningful, peace-filled, and happy life. En route to that is human sexuality. Honor your sexuality and your partner's, and you have a chance at great living. The Apostle Paul in I Corinthians 7:2 NIV says, "Each man should have his own wife, and each woman her own husband." Sex is not an amusement for the frivolous and irresponsible. It's a special joy to the responsible. Yes, have fun in courtship, love, marriage, and sex.

Fun Daily Among Basic Needs: Food, Clothing, and Shelter

Why not? How about a peanut butter and jelly sandwich on wheat bread? Caviar instead? Clam chowder is awesome too. All those fruits and vegetables at the super market: have you tried half of them? How many types and cuts of meat are there? How many types of seafood? How many cereals, candies, coffees? International cuisines: each has its specialties and you know they've stood the test of time. Greek, Scandinavian, Italian, French, German, Oriental. Simple tuna sandwiches and Pepsi Cola have been good for me for some time. I have a friend who must have his daily peanut butter and jelly. But we all do need to try new things too. It's time to eat, don't you think?

Clothing fun? Sure. Add a little color to your wardrobe. You've been conservative? Splash it up: magenta or turquoise. You've been very flashy? Try a mellow color: burgundy, cream, fuchsia, jade, or cranberry. You'll probably succeed in either direction. How about style? Loose-fitting, tailored, classical. How about fabric? Maybe silk-rayon, or velour. You've never been much for hats or scarves. Live a little more, try one. You may be amazed.

The point is: dare to have fun. Experiment. The Danforth Foundation put out a book entitled *I Dare You.* A daughter's high school friend dared recently at her inter-racial wedding to don with her husband, half way through the evening, Nigerian clothing! Again, what beautiful styles and colors each culture predicates itself upon! We can learn so much from each other if we'll just be receptive. And, oh, the fun.

Shelter? I wish each of us could have the knowledge, the time, and the wherewithal to design and build our own home. What fun! Most of us dabble at it with patios, decks, recreation room additions, another bedroom, etc. Some get their fun from interior decorating, painting or wallpapering, taking out a wall, turning regular windows into bay windows, etc. It is fun to create.

I am envious of Frank Lloyd Wright's tree inside a home. One story, two story, three story. Bungalow, duplex, triplex. Rambler, cabin, A-frame. And then there are mansions. The Vanderbilts, for instance: an eleven million dollar marble mansion, or a 70-room summer cottage. Extraordinary. But lest we become too provincial, shall we cross the ocean and check out mansions, palaces, and castles abroad? Mind-stretching. Incidentally, how about the fact that the above-mentioned palatial estates did not have the benefit of modern day financial "wizards," architects, mammoth construction companies, road builders and landscapers? And how about the engineering behind the pyramids? The world is indeed a melting pot of styles, fashions, tastes, and people. Foods, clothing, architecture: fun!

Hobbies and Free Time

Now, a more natural fun. Certainly, it should come naturally to us to find pleasure and enjoyment in recreation and leisure time activities. Take time for recreation. *Recreate*: what a great root word. "*Create again.*" Recreate your mind, body, and soul with fun-filled activities. It could be golf, boating, swimming, jogging, walking, biking, a health club, a racket club, a bridge club, a team (female-male-mixed, peanuts and mites to "Over 60," and "Over 70" teams). Recreate your being with recreation.

Recreate with a vacation. Take time for vacation. Even if it's only for forty-eight hours at a setting just 100 miles away. Familiarity of daily scene and routine breeds contempt or, at least, dullness. See some new sights. Do some new things. It will, in most cases, reenergize you upon return and deepen your appreciation for "Home." Even the brief getaways are like power naps; they invigorate. Even the single day without a balance of the physical, mental, and the spiritual is out of whack. How much more so a year without recreation-vacation. Remember, we're nothing without our health!

Let's consider one activity a little more specifically. I need to put in a plug for fishing. I think I've failed to utilize this great recreation enough in my life. Fishing is good. My first catch was a buffalo fish from a rural creek. Good. Bullheads were good. My daughter's first northern caught from a dock was good. When my wife Mamie was able to hook sixteen, eighteen, and twenty-one pound salmon in Alaska, nothing but good! And, ultimately for me, when I was able to fish rainbows or brown trout at dawn, mid-day, or evening in the streams of southeastern Minnesota, it was very good.

I'm dwelling on this because I believe I should have done it more. All of my fishing memories are positive. This book is about meaningful, satisfaction-filled living. I'm emphasizing it because I believe "the world" would be a better place for all of us if the common man and the aristocrat all regularly dropped a line in the water, honed their patience waiting for results, and let the breeze gently caress their cheeks. I, without a doubt, believe that if America's, China's, Ireland's, Palestine's, Israel's, Korea's, "Whoever's" world leaders went on annual week-long fishing trips together, there would be less chance we'd antagonize each other or attack each other.

As tour guide, I'd recommend we alternate countries. I am totally serious. The ambiance of a placid lake or a gurgling brook, the therapy of water lapping on a shoreline, the hypnotism of a mirror-like lake surface, fresh air and time, peace and patience: water therapy. A successful catch is a fringe benefit. The communion with Mother Nature and Creation is enough. There might be a 2½-pound rainbow, a twenty-nine inch walleye, or a twenty-four pound salmon. That's good too. Go fishing, at least a few times a year. Fishing is good for mind, body, and soul. It is good for peasant or politician!

Maybe it's the Walker Art Center for your free time. Perhaps your taste runs to *Showboat* at the Orpheum, *Hamlet* at the Guthrie, or *Cats* at the Ordway. These are local options. Your area has its own. Maybe it's live performance entertainment by individuals or groups. They may come to your area or maybe you travel to Nashville, Vegas, or elsewhere to see them. Maybe it's the VCR and your favorite videos. Maybe it's DVDs. Two all time great performers, Bob Hope and Lucille Ball, have recently left us. Purchase their classic videos. Maybe it's the cable and satellite television and all the possibilities from gardening to the History channel to the soaps to Biography to *A & E* to HBO to ESPN. Speaking of viewing: how about some leisure hours in those photo albums? Last, and, of course, not least, scoping the Internet has its attractions...and addicts.

Regardless, as the Beach Boys succinctly put it, "And, she'll have 'Fun-Fun-Fun' till her Daddy takes her T-Bird away." The bottom line is simply that man needs recreational time. Certainly, vacation if you can, but, assuredly, "recreation," if you can't, participant or spectator. Be good to yourself and try some new free time experiences. There are hosts of possibilities in the weekly Arts and Entertainment section of your newspapers.

Serving Is Fun!

My wife serves exceptional meals to visiting relatives and guests. She concludes the dining with large proportions of dessert delicacies. I know the preparation isn't all fun; however, the pride she takes in her efforts and the satisfaction she receives in appreciation from those who dine, are, I believe, fun for her.

It is fun to serve. It's more fun to serve than to be served. Do you remember the Dorothy Sayers, "More fun to punt, than be punted" axiom from earlier in this chapter? It's the same principle. As you have noted, I appreciate surprises. If we give surprises to others, or if we serve others, it is just the best.

The World War II blockbuster movie, *Saving Private Ryan,* asks a small group of soldiers to risk their lives behind enemy lines to save the last member of a set of four brothers, three of whom from this tragedy-plagued family have already been killed. Service! This young man, when found, rejects the "rescue" which would have freed him to go back to the States because he says he must serve his comrades who are in the same jeopardy as he is. Service!

My experience with serving others well, other than personal satisfaction which is enough in itself, has been the spoken thanks from the recipients and the unspoken thanks through looks and meaningful hugs. Either way, service is the equivalent of any other type of fun on the face of the earth! I kid you not. If your work world is service oriented, you've felt this when you've given your best. If you've belonged to service organizations, (Lions' Club, Jaycees, LINK, Masons, FCA), you've felt afterward what I have: that I've received much more back than I've ever given. If you volunteer to usher, to weekly care for a flower garden, to serve meals to street people, to help build homes in a Habitat for Humanity project: it's all the same. It's fun to help.

You're still uncertain if you can serve in these ways? There is another service that can be done by all. Psychologists, medical doctors, the clergy and beyond have all identified the therapeutic phenomenon of listening. You too can serve by simply being an understanding, compassionate listener. John Milton was right in his Sonnet 16: "They also serve who stand and wait." We all can serve by waiting and listening. Love others by listening. That is an invaluable service. My wife has this gift. She is a consummate listener: people want to talk to her. Strangers in an airport, on an elevator, in a mammoth department store, at a game: she's genuinely interested in sharing with others. Thus, they enjoy talking to her. If we're willing to listen, we can serve in this way every day.

Have the most fun in life by serving. Becoming like a servant is a power-laden life. Don't be afraid of having fun.

P.S. Miscellaneous fun:

1. Skipping stones on a pond or lake.
2. Feeling cool, fresh air caressing your skin and filling your nostrils and lungs.
3. Petting an animal.
4. Listening to a Baltimore oriole or a cardinal's song at sunset.
5. Reading and looking amazingly at your watch to discover you've read for two hours and five minutes...and it seemed but a short time ago that you had begun.
6. Stopping your car on a thoroughfare to allow a mother duck and her weaving entourage of eight ducklings to get across the street.

"And she had fun, fun, fun...until Daddy took her T-Bird away."

Every Day,
Every Millennium

Mother Earth

Dear God:

Thank-you for:

- Nurses, unlicensed angels.

- People who stoop to pet a dog's head.

- A biker who exercises his dog on a leash.

- Two cats in two house windows on opposite sides of the street, eyeing a dog walking down the same street.

- A young mother bearing her newborn on her stomach, kangaroo-pouch like, for a summer's walk to the library.

- Stoplights and rearview mirrors: the business man on the phone, the matron monitoring her makeup, the teenager singing and rocking.

- A 10-year-old helping a 6-year-old to follow the lyrics in a church hymnal.

- People of all races: all colors, all cultures, all climates, all ethnic backgrounds.

- Human capabilities: the moon, cures for dreaded diseases, computer chips, Bill Gates, Paul Allen, Michael Jordan, Tiger Woods, Mozart, Picasso, etc.

- Perspective: crutches, handicaps, cemeteries.

- Miracles of recovery of health, physical and mental.

- People who say "Thanks."

- People who are optimistic: "I'd go fishing for Moby Dick in a rowboat, and I'd bring the tartar sauce along."

- Smiles, none more perfect than that of an infant placidly awakening from a nap.
- The innocence of little children.
- The comfort and coziness of a warm bed.
- A gondola ride on a mountain slope.
- Music: singing, listening, playing, whistling... "A Candle in the Wind," "Golden Oldies," "How Great Thou Art," etc., etc., etc.

Thank you for giving us enjoyment through our five senses. The smile on the face of a loved one, the brilliance of a sunrise, the soft snow blanketing the evergreens after a gentle winter's dusting, or the poignancy of a Browning sonnet. The pleasure in the songs of cardinals, orioles, mourning doves, and humans. The sounds of babies gurgling or "talking," or the twilight's refrains from crickets, frogs, and pheasants. The warm, soft touch of a human being, the supple smoothness of leather, or the coolness of a marble coffee tabletop. The sweet taste of a bite of freshly baked apple pie, the mouth- watering goodness of a morsel/chunk of steak or lobster, or the candied excellence of your favorite milk chocolate. The smells of smoke from burning leaves, fragrance from a freshly blooming rose blossom, or the aromas of a special perfume or after-shave. Thank you, God, for our five senses.

Taste:

- New England Clam chowder.
- Aesop's bagels and Mango-Mama fruit juice.
- Orange popsicles on 98-degree temperature days.
- Children licking vanilla and chocolate cones at a Dairy Queen.

Smell:

- Thanksgiving turkey smells.
- Freshly mown alfalfa hay.
- The early morning smells of fresh, baked breads and rolls.

Sound:

- Sounds of a steady, gentle rain on the rooftop.
- Youthful cries and voices during recess at a school playground.
- A sandpiper's song at twilight as it protects its nest.
- Silence. Quiet.
- A mirror-like, still lake.
- The gentle lapping of waves on a rocky shoreline.
- A slow-moving stream and a rainbow trout jumping from the water.

Touch:

- A bath or a shower with soothing, relaxing hot water.
- A warm, moist pair of lips pressed upon yours.
- A reassuring pair of loving arms enclosing you in an embrace.

Sight:

- Fireflies.
- Fireworks.
- A hawk resting on a power line.
- A pigeon "floating" over a barn.
- A jet soaring through the stratosphere.
- Sunshine.
- Sunrises.
- Sundogs.
- Sun through the haze of snowflakes.
- Sunshine radiating through an A.M. shower into a puddle, reflected onto a shiny, metal overhang at a drive-in teller: "Ripples in the Wind."
- Awe-inspiring sunsets.
- Rainbows.

- Full moons on clear nights.

- 30 degrees and frosted trees of all types.

- Ethereal breaks of light through "mortal," cloudy skies.

Nathaniel Hawthorne said, "Our Creator would never have made such lovely days and given us the deep hearts to enjoy them, above and beyond all thought, unless we were meant to be immortal."

Thank you, Father.

Your Child

" *I've got peace like a river,*
I've got peace like a river,
I've got peace like a river in my soul. "

- Negro Spiritual

Epilogue

"Peace, like a river" is my favorite expression when saying good-by. I'll even use it towards only casual acquaintances. It works for me because it catches your ear and, I hope, catches your mind. It is a blessing. This book was written with the hope that your life might become more peace-filled as a result of "**becoming** something." The phrase, "Peace, like a river," I borrow from a Horatio Spafford song:

> When peace like a river, attendeth my way;
> when sorrows like sea billows roll;
> whatever my lot, thou hast taught me to say,
> It is well...it is well with my soul.
>
> Though Satan should buffet, though trials should come,
> let this blest assurance control:
> that Christ has regarded my helpless estate,
> and has shed his own blood for my soul.

My sin—O, the bliss of this glorious thought,
my sin—not in part, but the whole,
is nailed to the cross and I bear it no more:
Praise the Lord, praise the Lord, O my soul!

And, Lord, haste the day when my faith shall be sight,
the clouds be rolled back as a scroll,
the trump shall resound and the Lord shall descend:
"Even so"—it is well with my soul.

You and I with "Peace Like a River" in our souls are better prepared to deal with self, others, nature, and God. Listen, think, and practice the ideas shared here and you will experience peace. You will also have become the person you are meant to be.

I've got peace like a river, I've got peace like a river,
I've got peace like a river in my soul.

(Negro spiritual)